FEAR*LESS*

Shippensburg, PA

OTHER BOOKS BY CARLIE TERRADEZ

Miracles Made Easy: Inspiring Stories of Faith

Hannah and the Beanstalk! A True Story of Faith

ALSO FROM TERRADEZ MINISTRIES:

Thorns, Barns, and Oil Jars by Ashley Terradez

*Your Life with God: What it Means to Be Born Again
and Receive the Baptism of the Holy Spirit*

*39 Reasons Healing is Yours: Healing Scriptures
that Beat Sickness to Death*

FEAR*LESS*

BREAKING THE HABIT OF FEAR

CARLIE TERRADEZ

Published by Harrison House Publishers
Shippensburg, PA 17257

ISBN 13 TP: 978-1-6803-1750-3

ISBN 13 eBook: 978-1-6803-1751-0

ISBN 13 HC: 978-1-6803-1753-4

ISBN 13 LP: 978-1-6803-1752-7

For Worldwide Distribution, Printed in the U.S.A.

1 2 3 4 5 6 7 8 / 25 24 23 22 21

CONTENTS

FOREWORD

Fearless is a powerful book that is essential for the days in which we all live today. Carlie's personal victories will inspire you to run toward that giant called "fear" and cut off its ugly head. She has packed her book with practical steps that will show you how to break the fear habit and experience the kind of life that God called you to live. This timely book will challenge you to unleash the power of God in your life and run fearlessly toward your future.

—Cathy Duplantis

INTRODUCTION

You may not feel this right now. You may not even believe this right now. But, God created you to be bold, fearless, and intrepid.

You.

He created you to have a fearless mentality. Not to live in fear, not to be distracted by fear, but to walk into the fire of your struggle with courage. To stare it down until it flinches.

You.

I know it may not seem like that right now. Maybe that feels impossible right now. And, without God, it would be. With Him, though, all things are possible. That includes you over-coming your fears.

This is a personal topic for me. I understand fear, even irrational fear. I know how it can be the quiet voice in your head that dictates all your decisions. I know how it can limit you feeling free and unburdened. I know how you may hide it because it embarrasses you or scares you to admit it out loud.

I know because I've been there. I've allowed fear to be the captain at the helm. I gave up my freedom to decide what was best for my life, for my family, for a healthy mentality, and catered to whatever fear demanded.

Fear ruled. But God said, "No more."

As we take this journey together into the face of our fears, I want you to know there is liberty waiting for you at the end. Overcoming fear isn't for others only. It's for you, too. The power has been given to you by God.

Let's go claim it.

CHAPTER I

FEAR AND THE MONSTER WITH METAL TEETH

WHAT DO YOU FEAR?

For years, I feared escalators.

Does that seem irrational to you? To me, it was terrifying. Those metal steps. The jagged edges. The unstoppable motion. You have to step on, balance yourself, and wait expectantly for the end you know is coming. You know what I mean. The End. Where the step disappears underground and you barely escape being sucked in with it.

I hated them.

It started after an incident in a department store when I was five years old. While my mum shopped for clothes, I played and twirled and danced and ran around the top of an escalator.

"You stay away from the top of those stairs," Mum told me.

And I did. Until the moment I didn't. Instead of listening, I chose to play around the top of the escalators anyway. That's when I saw the handrail and grabbed on. Not realizing the handrail moved with the steps, I found myself being pulled with my feet still resting at the top of the stairs. Before I knew what was happening, I was yanked forward. I fell down the escalator and cut myself on the jagged metal steps.

It was a terrifying experience, and it stuck with me.

Through my childhood, through my teen years, into adulthood, I was still that scared, little girl crying out for her mother in fear and pain because of that metal monster.

After my husband, Ashley, and I got married and the kids were still small, we took a trip to London. Do you have any idea how inconvenient it is with buggies and strollers in the underground subway system in London when you can't take an escalator?

I would go further than I needed to go, walk longer than I needed to walk, make traveling more complicated than it needed to be, all to find an elevator. All so I could avoid the monsters. When that wasn't possible and one of those mammoth escalators was the only option, I would climb on and grip the handrails until my knuckles turned white. My heart would race. I'd start sweating. Then the dizziness would hit. It caused a full-on panic attack.

I was a grown woman still holding on to a child's fear that somehow, someway, I would fall again.

FEAR LIKE AN ESCALATOR

Our fears act exactly like that escalator, don't they? They suck us in, pull us down, and leave us terrified. And they're everywhere.

We can't get from where we are to where we want to go without being confronted with them constantly. To move forward, we have to face those fears, overcome those fears, maybe even use those fears to take us from here to there. To avoid them, we choose a lesser route or even a lesser destination.

If we've got to travel through, over, or with those fears to fulfill God's plan for our lives, maybe we'll just wait it out until He comes up with a *better* plan.

Right?

Sorry. It isn't going to work that way. Overcoming those fears may be the very thing God is going to use in your life to bless you beyond anything you could imagine. He is going to use you for His Kingdom in ways where you will know without a doubt it was God and God alone.

FEAR MAY HAVE YOU CHAINED NOW, BUT GOD SENT JESUS WITH BOLT CUTTERS

That fear may have you chained now, but God sent Jesus with bolt cutters! It's time to prepare for the freedom He wants you to experience.

THE MANY FACES OF FEAR

So, maybe you don't fear escalators. I hope you don't! The step's edges are like metal teeth. Did I mention the metal teeth?

Instead, your fear may be less around something that could happen to you and more around how people see you. You fear how you're perceived. You fear being ostracized or criticized or insulted. You fear people won't like you, won't esteem you, or will think ill of you.

That's the fear of man.

Or, maybe your fear is about want. You're worried God won't provide all your needs. You stress over the bills, over your responsibilities, over finding yourself without any means to take care of your family. You look at the future as something that is coming at you in attack mode. What will it bring? Will you be prepared?

That's the fear of lack.

Perhaps your fear is about the coming consequences of your actions. You know you've done something wrong or sinful. You stress and fret and twist yourself into all kinds of regret, while denying God's forgiveness. Even if you could finally forgive yourself, you know that second shoe is about to drop.

That's the fear of punishment.

People fear all kinds of different things, from the ultimate fear of death, the understandable fear of pain, to fearing abundance, attention, or popularity. If it's out there, we can find ways to fear it. But, why? Where does all this fear come from?

In 1 John 4:18, we read that *"perfect love casts out fear."* Ultimately, fear is a lack of faith. Deep down, though we mourn admitting it, we don't trust God to keep His Word. We doubt that God is good, that He is true to His Word, that He is with us, that He will never leave us, and that He has good for us. If we aren't completely captivated by the love of God, fear will play a predominant role in our lives.

What's worse, our fears may also play a predominate role in the lives of our loved ones.

FEAR IS CONTAGIOUS

During a conference in Arizona, a man approached me to lay hands on him for his wife. She couldn't come down from her hotel room to receive the healing she desperately needed, so he wanted me to lay hands on him so he could go upstairs and lay hands on her.

"She's in bed in the hotel room because she's incapacitated. She's bed-bound. She's unable to come down to receive prayer," he said. "I want you to lay your hands on me so that the power of God is in me, and I can go lay hands on my wife."

That's how he was believing, and that's how he wanted to receive.

As I placed my hands on him for prayer, the Holy Spirit checked me. God was letting me know there was more to the story here. I heard His still, small voice tell me to look at the man. Instantly, I knew what the Lord wanted me to see. This husband was in desperate fear of losing his wife.

"You know what? What I'm sensing when I'm looking at you is fear," I told him.

In the midst of that prayer for healing for his wife, I also spoke the peace of God over him to counteract his fear. In that moment, you could see his body relaxing. The fear, that only moments earlier I could see in his eyes and posture, was leaving.

He appreciated the prayer and left. I didn't think any more about it until hours later when I ran into him again. He looked completely different. In fact, his countenance had changed so much, I didn't even recognize him.

"You don't recognize me, do you?" he asked. "You prayed for me this morning. I'm the man with the fear. Well, I want to introduce you to someone. This is my wife."

She stood beside him looking healthy, happy, and simply radiant. He told me that after the prayer, as he was in the elevator going back to his room, the power of God hit his wife in her bed and all her symptoms left. All her pain was gone and her mobility returned!

Fear had kept this woman in bondage.

She had been struggling to believe God for her healing and wean herself off medication. She had been taking steps forward in faith, but her husband's fear was keeping her bound. He loved her so much that his fear had kept her from stepping out in faith.

His sympathy was—literally—loving her to death. When the fear was finally broken in his life, the power of God was able to flow, and she received her healing.

When you have a spouse or loved one who is ill, it's natural to feel fear and trepidation. You're worried and anxious. Every day, you're fighting off the fear of what might happen. These emotions are natural and expected. When our daughter was given a week to live, I had them all.

But we can't just stop feeling. That's not the answer. It isn't even possible. We are going to have fear. Fear of what might happen. Fear for them. Even fear for how their illness will change our lives, too.

This can be especially tormenting when a family member suffers from an illness that could be hereditary. Not only are you watching that disease attack them and hating to see them in pain while stressed over providing them care, you also know in the back of your head it could eventually be you.

That's a potent fear that can grip us at a time when we're already exhausted, emotionally drained, and susceptible to stress.

So, what do we do?

We make the choice to not allow fear to drive us. We must always stop our fear before it becomes the predominant emotion in our life. We must deny our fears any authority. They may exist, but they don't need to be in the lead.

FEAR OF THE UNKNOWN

Ashley tells this story about a school experience that perfectly illustrates how his fear of what *could* happen was so much worse than what actually *did* happen:

> When I was in school, there was this big kid who I offended somehow. I don't know how, exactly, but it was enough that he decided to beat me up after school. That day, everyone was talking about it. Other kids kept coming up to me and saying, "He's going to deck you after school. Just wait. He's going to beat you up."
>
> All day, that's all I could think about. This guy was coming for me. He was bigger than me, tougher than me, and he wanted me to pay. I imagined exactly what was coming for me. All day, through all my classes, all I could think about was that dreaded moment.
>
> Eventually, the school day ended and I had to go face this guy. I'd worked myself up imagining what was coming. Walking into that school yard, I felt my terror in every step.
>
> Once I got there, the guy stomped toward me and punched me once. Then he said, "Now, don't say that again," and walked off. All I could think was, Is that it?

It was no big deal. It didn't even hurt. All day, I'd been trembling over what was coming to me when that final bell rang, and it turned out my fear leading up to the event was far worse than the event itself.

My dear Ashley. He's a lover not a fighter.

Fear often starts small. It's a small seed, a small thought. Then, as time goes on, as you give it more focus, you water that fear and it grows. You waste your time thinking about it. You spend your energy obsessing over it. You forfeit your productivity in other areas to allocate more effort to cater to it. And all it does is grow. The more it grows, the more you feed it. The more you feed it, the bigger it grows. Before long, it's gotten so big it can crowd out the light.

FEAR BECOMES FALSE EVIDENCE APPEARING REAL

We find ourselves fearing, even to an irrational degree, something that may not even be true. Fear becomes **False Evidence Appearing Real**. And we can't convince ourselves otherwise.

FIGHT FEAR WITH FAITH

Fear, of the known or unknown, of the real or imagined, works to paralyze us with the threat of "the possibilities." We become stuck—unable to move forward, unable to overcome, unable to stop feeding the monster we've created.

Now what? Are we doomed to fear?

Satan would love nothing more than to convince you that your fear is insurmountable. Never forget, his sole purpose is to steal, kill, and destroy (John 10:10). He steals our peace. He kills our hope. He destroys our joy.

But that's not the end of our story. God is the author here, and He's the ender of all fear. That includes your fear, too.

Here's how we fight fear with faith:

I. TAKE CONTROL OF YOUR THOUGHT LIFE

Our thought life affects every other aspect of our lives. The more time we spend thinking of things that do not produce life, the more our lives will be eroded. Scripture tells us that out of the abundance of our hearts our mouths speak (Luke 6:45; Matthew 12:34). When we're consumed with fear, we talk about it. We internalize and verbalize it. Before long, our words become toxic, reflecting our toxic thoughts.

If you're consumed with worst case scenarios, with always finding the negative, with focusing on anything fearful you can find in every situation, you will give your life over to your fears.

2. CALL THAT WHICH IS EVIL, EVIL

In Romans 12:21, Paul writes, *"Do not be overcome by evil, but overcome evil with good."* The fear we're talking about truly is evil. It is robbing us of peace and attacking our joy.

God wants us to trust Him, but we cannot trust Him while cowering in fear. The two simply cannot coexist. When we walk with Christ, we will never walk in fear.

3. LOOK FEAR IN THE EYE

I know this is going to be hard, but you've got to face down that fear. You do that by asking yourself one simple question, "What's the worst that could happen?"

When I was struggling with my escalator fears, I had to come to terms with the ultimate scenario. What happens if I trip and fall? I'll hurt myself, but I will survive. In fact, it probably won't even be all that bad.

With other fears, however, the worst thing that could happen is far greater. In fact, it may even result in death. How do we face fear like that?

POWER OVER DEATHLY FEAR

You may be fearing a sickness right now or even the possibility of an illness. You may be waiting on a doctor's report, and, depending on what it says, you could be facing the ultimate battle with fear. If you are sick, will it be painful? If you need treatment, will it be available? If there is no treatment, are you going to die?

Maybe it's not an illness but a devastating financial loss. Will you and your family go without? Will there still be food to eat? Will your family starve? Or go homeless?

Perhaps you fear being outcast from society. Will you be alone? Will you lose your job? Your friends? Your community?

Ultimately, all these fears can be traced to the fear of death, either literally or as the death of something beloved. The Lord, however, has something better for us than death.

In Hebrews 2:14, we see how Jesus approached death:

> *So then, as the children share in flesh and blood, He* [Jesus] *likewise took part in these, so that through* [His] *death He might destroy him who has the power of death, that is, the devil, and deliver those who through fear of death were throughout their lives subject to bondage* (MEV, brackets added).

The devil once had the power of death. That power is no more.

You see, fear keeps people in bondage, but Jesus says here He's come to deliver us from the fear of death and living in bondage. He has better plans for us than to live in fear. That first step out of fear begins with courage.

TIME TO BE BOLD

The Lord repeatedly told Joshua, "Do not be afraid" (Joshua 1:6-9). Why would He say that? Could it be that Joshua, the mighty warrior, was fighting fear?

One of the things we learn about Joshua's life was that he was always fighting people. He was always in one scrape or another, one battle or another, one insurmountable challenge or another.

As the successor to Moses as the leader of the children of Israel, Joshua was tried and tested, sometimes by his own people, sometimes from outside sources. Moses left big sandals to fill, and Joshua must have frequently felt the heaviness of that responsibility and those expectations. He may have even doubted himself.

God saw his challenges and responded by commanding Joshua to only "be strong and courageous."

The Lord is never going to ask us to do something that He hasn't already given us the ability to do. When Jesus told the disciples many times, "Do not fear," or when Jesus told a dying girl's father, "Do not fear, only believe," that's because He had equipped them with His strength and power to do exactly what He was commanding. He had given them the ability to not fear. That same ability is also for us so that we can take power over our anxious thoughts, apply truth, and move forward without fear but with faith.

Fear is part of the curse, but we've been redeemed from that curse. In the same way we can look to God for the forgiveness of our sin and the healing of our body, we find in Him the power to overcome fear.

THE LORD DOESN'T ASK YOU TO DO SOMETHING HE HASN'T ENABLED YOU TO DO

PERFECT LOVE ENDS FEAR

Jesus doesn't want us to live with fear. He wants us to have the same hatred for fear that we do for sickness or poverty or injustice or anything else He atoned for through His sacrifice. He wants us to cast off the fear that torments us by being confident in His love.

*We have come into an intimate experience with God's love, and **we trust in the love He has for us**. God is love! Those who are living in love are living in God, and God lives through them. By living in God, love has been brought to its full expression in us **so that*** *we may fearlessly face the day of judgment, because all that Jesus now is, so are we in this world* (1 John 4:16-17 TPT, emphasis added).

When we come to know and really believe the love that God has for us, it changes us. You see that happening in verse 17, and in the Modern English Version it reads, *"In this way God's love is perfected in us, so that we may have boldness..."*

Remember, one of the characteristics of being fearless is being bold. It's being brave. It's being intrepid. The passage goes on to say, *"...that we might have boldness on the Day of Judgment, because as He [Jesus] is, so are we in this world. There is no fear in love, but perfect love casts out fear"* (brackets added).

God's love is the antidote to any fears that we might have in our lives.

Fear left unchecked will torment us. It will hold us in bondage, but 1 John 4:18 continues, *"Whoever fears is not perfect in love."* God loves us so much that He paid the ultimate price to free us from bondage and torment.

Don't let the devil rent space in your head by suggesting unfounded fear that's based on lies or by magnifying a negative experience out of proportion. Satan once had the power of death, but Jesus defeated his power. Be confident that the enemy no longer has power in your life. The only power he has is what you give him when you do not place your trust in God's Word.

Reject your fear and embrace your freedom.

CHAPTER 2

PICKING A FIGHT WITH FEAR

ARE YOU LIVING FEARLESSLY?

When given an option to rank your fears, studies have proven most people will list public speaking before death. Imagine that! Between the option of standing on a stage to deliver a talk or jumping off a cliff, many would gaze longingly at the cliff.

Fear of public speaking is so tormenting, so horrifying, they fear it more than the loss of their life! They fear *the fear* more than *the result.*

That's the power of our fears. And that's what God will defeat for us.

How?

It happened on the cross. We talk a lot about the promises God has given us—about receiving forgiveness, health, and prosperity—but how often do we talk about the power to over-come our fears? We have that as a promise, too. The deliverance from all fear was paid for by Jesus.

Do you want to live boldly? Do you want to feel brave? Do you want to live fearlessly? When we fully understand what Jesus did for us, we can live a renewed freedom. We can walk with security and confidence, without fear.

It's a promise from God. And it's time we believed it.

TAKE THE STAGE

Remember those people who feared public speaking? Well, that's this girl. Right here. It terrified me. And there was no way to escape.

While attending Bible college, we were all given the assign-ment of a ten-minute public talk on a verse out of Philippians. They told us about this assignment on the first day of school. So, I knew it was coming. And I was absolutely terrified.

I knew it was illogical. Fearing dath or fearing pain or fear-ing the loss of a loved one, that made sense. Fearing public speaking did not. But there I was being completely illogical—and petrified.

Knowing it was coming, I decided it would be better to sign up to be one of the first to speak instead of sitting through thirty other people speaking, all while I grew more and more nervous. If I got mine out of the way, I could relax.

Right? Right?!

JUMP OFF THE CLIFF

On a ministry trip to South Africa, our family went paragliding. It wasn't planned at all. One minute we're ministering at a church, the next we're jumping off a mountain.

I don't know how that happened.

The pastor at the church where we were ministering apparently overheard one of our kids mentioning how fun it would be to paraglide, and I—not realizing I was signing over my life in that moment—agreed.

When we finished ministering, the pastor invited us into his car and off we went. Of course, Ashley and I thought he was just taking us to lunch! That's usually what happens. But, nope. He decided to "gift" us with a paragliding adventure.

So, we drove up this mountain and, the next thing we know, we've signed disclaimers and they're outfitting us in equipment. When I realized I was up first, I said, "What? Me first? Let me go say goodbye to my family!"

Real woman of faith and power right there.

Knowing that the edge awaited me, knowing there was no way out of it, knowing the fear would never relent, knowing this wasn't the lunch I'd hoped for—I ran with the instructor anyway, and we jumped off the mountain.

It was incredible.

I'm so glad I did it. It was an experience I will never forget. The memory of that day could have been one of fear and anxiety, but because I didn't let fear win, I have a treasured memory of a joy-filled thrill.

FACE THE FEAR

Not every fear requires leaping from a mountain top to be tamed. Sometimes—most times—it simply requires you face it head on. Like my ten-minute talk in Bible college.

Instead of running from it, I ran toward it. But not before God gave me a stern talking to about His plan and my plan and which one needed to change. He showed me that He had called me to teach and preach in front of people.

I, of course, argued with Him over this. I didn't want to do it.

You see, Ashley is the life of the party. He's the one with the funny stories. I'm the one laughing at them. He's Mr. Big Personality. I'm Mrs. Introvert. He's exuberant. I'm happy to live in a cabin in the woods.

What I saw for my future was to be Ashley's support. He could do the ministering. I could make the coffee.

God had other plans.

"Listen," I told God, "Ashley's your man. I'm the support personnel. I'll be the backup team."

The Lord, in reply, laid it out pretty straight with me. "You don't want to do this because you're afraid to do this. Are you seriously not going to do what I've called you to do? Are you not going to fulfill the plans and purposes I have for your life simply because you're afraid?"

That hit me at a heart level.

God was telling me that fear was only an emotion, an emotion He could free me from and give me control over. I wanted the fear to go away first, but God was saying He would give me the courage to do whatever He called me to do.

I was afraid to do it. But God said, "Do it afraid."

I WAS AFRAID TO DO IT. BUT GOD SAID, "DO IT AFRAID."

FAITH VERSUS FEAR

Once I accepted that fear would be part of the process, God directed me forward. I made a commitment to Him that the next time I had an opportunity to speak, I would say yes. And I'd keep saying yes every time the opportunity came.

The minute I agreed to face my fear, it made me trust God because I knew I could not do it in the flesh, in the natural, in my own strength.

That's where faith and fear collide. They are complete opposites. Fear paralyzes us from moving; faith strengthens us to forge ahead.

In 1 John, we read about the torment of fear. It overwhelms us to the point we completely stop. We stop doing things, stop acting, stop taking the opportunities in front of us. Faith, however, undoes all that fear damage. It motivates us. It activates us. It gives us the power to take those opportunities when they come.

Fear isn't going to go away, or even be placed in the background, without a fight. Get ready to rumble because it will war with you: mentally and physically. You will need to throw yourself on the Lord. You will need His help to overcome it.

Facing my fear of public speaking wasn't a passive activity. It was a high-intensity workout! It was a battle in my mind. I had to ask myself some serious questions and seek my heart for the answers.

Did I believe God was bigger than this situation? Did I believe He was big enough to come through for me? Did I trust Him to protect me from shame, embarrassment, and people's opinions even if I messed up? Did I believe He was big enough to deal with my heart if the circumstances turned ugly?

I had to give God His rightful dominion over the consequences. When we operate in fear, the consequences are our responsibility. When we operate in faith, they are God's.

I would much rather have God be responsible for the consequences of my actions when I'm operating in faith than me being responsible for them when I'm operating in fear.

FIGHTING ON THE FRONTLINES

Making a decision to move forward in faith is the first, and most crucial, step toward living fearlessly. But it isn't the last. You still have to get into the fight.

Confronting what's coming will be easier now because you've got security. God will be with you. Remember, He's the one responsible for the consequences, but you've still got to step onto the battlefield.

When I started accepting public speaking opportunities, I had to contend with the realities of my fear. As I prepared my message, my mind would trigger a physical response. My flesh would rise up. My heart would beat faster. Adrenaline would shoot into my system. I'd wrestle with that fight or flight instinct.

You know what I'm talking about.

The moment your mind starts to fear, your body doesn't try to talk your mind out of it. It goes along to get along. It jumps on board. It even offers to drive.

In your mind, you start hearing all these sirens going off: "You're going to perish. You're going to perish. You. Are going. TO PERISH." You worry you'll pass out, and you feel yourself starting to pass out. You fear you'll get tongue-tied, and you start getting tongue-tied.

I get it because I've been there. When I was living in fear, I just took it. When I decided to live in faith, I started talking back, literally.

"Shut up, flesh. Listen to me. This is what we're going to do, and I don't care if you like it or not. You can have your hissy fit elsewhere. I'm not letting you keep me from what God's called me to do. I'm not going to let this emotion rent space in my head."

Panic was trying to take over, and I had to confront it. Instead of letting it be the master, I started speaking to my body. I told my adrenaline, "Calm yourself down," and my racing heart, "Settle." And my body started to listen.

The more I practiced addressing my body and not concentrating on my fear, the less I felt that emotion and the less those physical symptoms appeared. That cycle of fear ended more quickly.

WHEN FEAR BECOMES REALITY

Unlike me, Ashley never feared public speaking. He comes alive out there. But that doesn't mean he doesn't also contend with fear. We all do! Every one of us. Even confident gents like my husband. For Ashley, his fear actually happened in the most inopportune moment. It was adorable, but *he* didn't think so. I'll let him tell you about it:

> I fear making a fool of myself. It has hindered me from saying yes to things because I think, *What if I mess up and get made fun of?* Well, my fear actually

came true, back when Carlie and I were dating, when I met her friends for the first time.

We joined her church youth group and some of her other friends I hadn't met—about 25 of them—for a game of 10-pin bowling. Here was my issue: I had to make a good first impression and I feared I wouldn't. So, I chose my clothes carefully, which was a pair of baggy jeans. (Hey, it was 20-years ago. They were super fashionable.) And, we went bowling.

When we got there, we were late. Everyone else was already there and had everyone's names programmed into the game. They were ready to go and, of course, my name came up first. 'A' for Ashley, I guess.

I stepped up, knowing this was my chance to make a good first impression.

It's important to understand here that I knew nothing about bowling. So, I chose the heaviest bowling ball I could find. I could barely lift it, but I was out to impress. I knew I had to make this good. I thought, *If I can make a strike on my first bowl, they'll be wowed. They'll be really impressed by this man of God that Carlie is going to marry.*

I stepped onto the lane carrying the heaviest bowling ball I could find and wearing the most fashionable baggy jeans I own. I was ready to impress. So, I gave it everything I had.

That's when it all went wrong.

My thumb got stuck in the bowling ball, which messed up my release, and then I slipped on my baggy jeans. The ball ended up flying down the lane the wrong way and heading into the crowd. I ended up on my face sliding toward the pins. I made it halfway down the lane before I stopped!

In that moment, I remember laying there thinking, *This is the worst first impression I could possibly make.* It was awful, but you know what? It wasn't as bad as I'd feared. Yet again, the something bad actually happening was less tormenting than the fear of something bad happening.

How does the story end? I still got the girl!

POWER OVER THE WORST

When you think about your worst fears, they seem insurmountable, don't they? How do you ever stop fearing illness? Or loss? Or, the worst of them all, death? How do you get to a place in life where the idea of dying or losing a loved one doesn't immediately strike panic?

With man, it would not be possible. But, with God, all things are possible. All things. Even this.

Overcoming your fears is not about dismissing or belittling them. These are reasonable, honest, and universal fears. They're real. They're frightening. They're serious situations. Getting power over our fears isn't about minimizing their reality but putting that reality into a godly perspective.

> GETTING POWER OVER OUR FEARS ISN'T ABOUT MINIMIZING THEIR REALITY BUT PUTTING THAT REALITY INTO A GODLY PERSPECTIVE

As born-again Christians, we have a future that does not need to be feared. In truth, we can't lose for winning. When something bad comes into our lives, we are still in the hands of God. That means when illnesses come, we can go to our loving Father for healing and wholeness. Even if the worst possible outcome happens, we have an eternity with Jesus waiting.

In every situation in life, wherever we are in need, God is with us. He will provide. We're safe with Him.

Believing this is how we stop giving fear any authority. But that believing part is a bit like climbing Mt. Everest, right?

FEAR'S POWER DENIED

God has broken fear for you already. Did you know that? He removed its authority when He redeemed us from the curse.

In Deuteronomy 28, we learn about the curses Christ overcame on the cross and the blessings He offers us today. Verses 1 through 14 show us all the blessings God's children can receive today, while verses 15 onward illustrate all the things Jesus redeemed for us by the shedding of His blood.

As we go down the chapter, we come to verse 66, which will give us a fresh perspective on our fear:

> *Your life shall hang in doubt before you; you shall fear day and night, and have no assurance of life.*

Doesn't this sound terrible?

Hold on. We're not done. This is a journey and our next stop is new eyes to see. Look at verse 67:

> *In the morning you shall say, 'Oh, that it were evening!' And at evening you shall say, 'Oh, that it were morning'…*

In other words, no matter where we find ourselves, we'll find reasons to be dissatisfied. We're always trying to be somewhere else because we think somewhere else will be better. Why are we so dissatisfied?

...because of the fear which terrifies your heart, and because of the sight which your eyes see.

Galatians 3:13 says Jesus redeemed us from the curse of the law. When you read chapter 28 of Deuteronomy today, only the blessings apply. Every curse has been cancelled. No more terror at what our eyes see or our hearts feel. No more wishing to avoid our lives and be somewhere or someone else. No more unsettling dissatisfaction.

Fear is part of the curse that no longer has any right to us. We are redeemed.

POWER OVER THE MIND'S EYE

When my babies were toddlers, they caught a terrible bug. It was awful. The sickness. The diarrhea. The laundry to keep up. I was running from one disaster to the next.

Moms, you know what I mean.

During all this, I woke up one night at one in the morning with my stomach churning, the room spinning, and a sickness setting in. The symptoms were all there, right down to the sweats and stomach pain.

Off to the bathroom I went. And it wasn't pretty. Let's just say, I did not look like a woman of faith and power at that moment.

With the trash can positioned strategically in front of me, butt on the throne, and my entire body ready to heave, I suddenly realized I had power in this situation.

"I'm going to speak to these symptoms," I told myself, "and I'm going to get my faith on. This is all going to subside. All these symptoms are going to stop."

I bound and loosed—literally. I spoke in power. I commanded my guts to calm down!

And nothing. No change.

So, I asked the Lord, "What is it? I'm doing what I know to be doing. I know life and death are in the power of the tongue. I'm commanding, binding, and loosing, aren't I? Why isn't this working?"

God spoke to me and said, "It's because you're afraid."

He showed me I already had history with this illness. I had days and days of seeing it play out with my babies. The sickness. The diarrhea. All the consequences. I was overwhelmed by the fear in my heart.

In my mind, I was already imagining myself with those symptoms, and I was overwhelmed with the fear of the consequences coming. I was already making plans to manage those consequences, like taking the next day off work and getting help with the kids.

It was subtle, but my mind was already playing through how I would manage the flu. The problem is we aren't designed to *manage* but to *believe*.

FAITH SEES HOPE

Fear is the opposite of faith. Where fear paints a bleak picture, faith illustrates all that is possible. Where fear focuses on destruction, faith strategizes for a positive future.

Even though the words I was speaking to my trash can were good, there was no faith behind them. In 2 Corinthians 4:13, it says we believe and, therefore, we speak. Sometimes we may find ourselves saying all the right things, but not believing them because of our fear.

I've seen this from believers in all kinds of ministry situations. Many times, their prayer turns into frantically chanting, "In the name of Jesus. In the name of Jesus. In the name of Jesus." They are allowing fear to be their motivator. When that happens, they see lots of activity, lots of torment, and no results.

However, when faith is our motivator, we have peace.

WE MAY FIND OURSELVES SAYING THE RIGHT THINGS, BUT NOT BELIEVING THEM OUT OF FEAR

Maybe, like me, you've found yourself saying all the right things and seeing no change or no answer. It wasn't until I realized all my binding and loosing was still rooted in fear that I found my faith. That's when things turned around.

In minutes, the symptoms left.

FEAR'S ANTIDOTE

John 16:33 is what I like to call "fear's antidote." In this verse, Jesus says,

> *I have told you these things, so that in Me you may have [perfect] peace and confidence. In the world you have tribulation and trials and distress and frustration...*

Here's the part where hope walks through the door:

> *...but be of good cheer [take courage; be confident, certain, undaunted]!*

That is how we'd describe being fearless, isn't it?

> *For I have overcome the world. [I have deprived it of power to harm you and have conquered it for you]* (AMPC).

I love that. When we're operating in faith rather than fear, we can acknowledge that we may feel fear in the flesh because it's based on real circumstances. However, we choose faith instead. We choose not to dwell on that fear, but to put our trust and confidence in God.

In our own strength, we could not do this. But, we're not in our own strength! We're trusting in God's confidence, God's boldness, and God's strength. Thank you, Lord, for depriving the world of the power to harm me!

JUST A DEMON

Years ago, I was leading a team of Bible college students on a mission trip to Russia. We were to host a pastors' conference, with men and women coming from all over Russia to join us. The night before the big event, the team stayed in various houses in a small village in a remote part of the country.

I was staying in a home with one of my co-leaders and a woman with a three-month-old baby. In the middle of the night, around one in the morning, there was a knock at my bedroom door. The other leader woke me because something was wrong with the little baby boy. They'd been praying and praying and hoped I could help.

We headed to another room where the baby's mother held the small child as he cried and cried. This was not a typical fussy cry or even a cry of pain. I could feel right away that there wasn't a medical issue or physical problem with the child. Healing was not what he needed.

I could sense in my spirit that there was a demonic presence in the room, and it was tormenting the sweet baby. Together, we all read and spoke out Psalm 91, just one simple yet powerful psalm. Instantly, peace came over the room and the boy fell asleep in his mother's arms. I thought, *Cool. That's dealt with.*

I went back to my own bedroom, and the moment I walked in I felt something very different in the space than when I'd left. It was incredibly cold. A chill was in the air like an icy frost. I snuggled myself deep under my covers, trying find some warmth.

The room was also terribly dark, so dark I couldn't see my hand in front of my face. As I lay in bed, trying to warm up and get some sleep, I felt a cold jet stream run through my body like an ice cube on my spine.

An impossible heaviness came over me, like the deep darkness of the room was trying to get on the inside of me. I was greatly disturbed. I sat up in bed and, even through the darkness of the night, I saw a presence of even deeper darkness in the corner of the room.

Fear gripped me. This darkness, this presence, this sense of absolute despair suddenly tried to get on the inside of me. I could feel my heart racing, not sure what to do.

"Lord, what is this?" I asked Him. "What is this that I'm feeling? What is this presence? What's going on here?"

The Lord spoke to me, and He said, "It's just a demon."

"Oh," I repeated the Lord's words to me out loud, "It's just a demon."

At those simple words, that change in perspective, all the heaviness left. The dark, scary demon was just a conquered foe, deprived of its power to harm me. I rolled over and went to sleep.

OVERPLAYING ITS HAND

Fear will always overplay its hand. The enemy will always try to appear bigger, more scary, and more intimidating than the beat-down loser he really is. I guess there's not a lot of subtlety in a demon.

Sometimes fear comes on suddenly as a demonic manifestation. It doesn't connect to your train of thought or relate to past experiences and phobias. It just floods your mind all at once, out of nowhere. You may feel something physical like goosebumps or a spike in your heart rate.

That's just satan being dramatic.

But the peace of God lives inside of us. We carry God's power in us. His Word is alive in us. We have nothing to fear from silly, overdramatic demons and their showy displays.

The Word of God is the cure for any demonic manifestation of fear. That night, the Holy Spirit showed me this was "just a demon." As soon as I measured that dark presence up against Jesus, it lost all its power. Just a few words from Psalm 91, just a shift in perspective in my heart, and both the baby and I were sleeping peacefully, free from fear.

WE HAVE NOTHING TO FEAR FROM SILLY, OVERDRAMATIC DEMONS AND THEIR SHOWY DISPLAYS

INTERRUPT THE INTERRUPTION

The next day, my team and I led an incredible conference with pastors from all over Russia. It was a powerful time of ministry, but we didn't have enough translators.

Miraculously, the Holy Spirit filled me with the ability to understand Russian. I couldn't speak Russian, but I could understand it for those hours while I needed that ability to hear and understand the language. As people came up for prayer, I understood every word they said and knew how to pray for their needs.

I'd never heard of the gift of interpretation of a known language. It blew my mind! I didn't know that could happen!

Later, when our team who had spent the night split up in separate houses finally had a chance to gather, we realized many of us had experience demonic manifestations the night before. For some it was fear or anxiety, others had random sickness or saw physical manifestations.

Clearly, the enemy wanted to interrupt the move of God that was underway with our event. We even learned that the area was steeped in witchcraft, and the local witches had gathered that night specifically because "the Christians" were in town.

Knowing what we have inside of us, knowing every curse has been broken, knowing Jesus has overcome the world allowed each member of the team to shut out fear in any form. We don't have to be afraid of any of the evil in this world. We have a refuge in our mighty God (Psalm 91:4)!

CHAPTER 3

FEAR "IN THE BEGINNING"

IS FEAR ACCUSING YOU?

A pastor friend of ours took his four-year-old daughter to the supermarket. Anytime you take a four-year-old to the supermarket, you know an unknown adventure awaits.

While they were shopping, she asked her dad for candy. Being the responsible parent, he told her, "No, we're not buying that today."

That's when the simple trip to the grocery store turned into a declaration of war.

His daughter, refusing to accept his answer, threw herself on the ground and proceeded to throw a full-on—in technicolor and surround sound—hissy fit. She banged her fists on the floor. She kicked her feet. She wailed and cried and screamed.

That kid wanted candy.

Her dad stood in the middle of the grocery store, knowing everyone watching was making their own assumptions about his parenting skills. So, he went into action. He threw himself on the ground beside her and threw a hissy fit, too.

His daughter didn't see that coming.

Suddenly, she calmed herself, stood up, looked down at her father and said, "Daddy, get up. You're embarrassing me."

Isn't that just like fear? It stands there in judgment. It preys on our insecurities, our failings, our weaknesses, our short-falls. Fear acts like this because fear is from the devil. He is the author of lies. He's the accuser of the brethren. And he accuses us with fear.

How many times have you heard that accusatory voice in your head whispering, "You can't do it. You're not strong enough. You're not smart enough. You don't have the resources. Look at the mess you've made."

Satan doesn't stop there, either. Once the thought is planted, he works feverishly to throw all our mistakes, our shame, and our guilt directly into our faces.

"What will other people think about you?" He leans in even closer, "You're embarrassing yourself."

Christ silences the accuser.

OUT OF FOCUS

Fear puts the focus on us, but faith puts the focus on God. We can do nothing without Christ, but we can do everything with Him. When our focus is on God and Christ in us, our eyes look to the One that fear cannot touch.

Jesus is clear about how we should view fear. In 2 Timothy 1:7, we're told, *"For God has not given us a spirit of fear, but of power and of love and of a sound mind."*

Fear has no place in the heart of a believer. Why? Because God loves us so much, He frees us to not only come to Him but also to come boldly. To approach Him without an ounce or trace of fear.

That is complete intimacy.

Fear wants to destroy that intimacy, not only with God but with others, too. It makes us hold people at arm's length or put on a mask to hide ourselves. Fear will change how we act or what we say. And, if we're not careful, we'll act one way in public and another way at home.

Allowing fear of man, fear of failure, and fear of rejection to creep into our lives will make us two different people: one public and one private.

It often happens subtly.

We can have these secret motivations, things we don't even realize, that affect us from past experiences. For example, if we had a parent who let us down, we may view our heavenly Father like our earthly father. Without us even realizing it, that experience creates fear in our soul that stops us from trusting God the way we want to trust Him.

That's where the enemy will create negative, fearful thoughts for us to meditate on.

THE GREAT EXCHANGE

In Isaiah 53, we read about Jesus' coming. It's a short chapter but so powerful. In it, we learn what Jesus was going to do and what He was going to redeem us from: *"Surely He has borne our griefs and carried our sorrows"* (Isaiah 53:4).

The word "grief" is key. The Hebrew word is *choli,* which means sickness, calamity, and anxiety. The word "sorrows" is *makob,* which means pain, anguish, and affliction. So, not only does this verse cover pain and affliction, it also covers the loss of mental peace.

Verse 5 then goes on to say, *"But he was wounded for our transgressions, He was bruised for our iniquities; the chastisement for our peace was upon Him, and by His stripes, we are healed."*

Jesus took our grief, our sorrow, and our anxiety at the cross. That's the Gospel. He took all of our pain and, in return, we get His health, healing, wholeness, and peace. It is the great exchange.

He redeemed us from it all, including the fear that is hindering us. 1 John 4:18 says that fear is a torment. Jesus came to end that torment and replace it with a new life free of anxiety.

> # HE TOOK ALL OF OUR PAIN AND, IN RETURN, WE GET HIS HEALTH, HEALING, WHOLENESS, AND PEACE. IT IS THE GREAT EXCHANGE.

MIND SET FREE

Many people struggling with mental illness find the root of their trouble in fear. Proverbs 12:25 says, *"Anxiety in the heart of man causes depression."* And Proverbs 23:7 tells us that as a man thinks in his heart, so he is.

When we plant a seed of fear, fear will take root in our hearts.

It may start with a traumatic experience, a harsh word, or a painful time. We take that into our heart and meditate on it. Doing this feeds that seed. It magnifies that experience or word or pain because anything we think about or meditate on will always become bigger.

Now we've got worry blooming and depression sprouting. From that initial seed comes all kinds of mental illness that prospers in that environment.

In chapter one, we talked about the fear of death and how Jesus has delivered us from this fear (Hebrews 2:14-15). For believers, death has no power.

Unless we believe that, we'll continue to live in fear's bondage. And that's what Isaiah 53 is talking about. No one can break the bondage of fear in our lives but Jesus. And He has done it. He took that bondage far from us. It's gone. Erased. Finito.

In Acts 2:24, we learn more about Jesus' resurrection: "[Jesus] *Whom God raised up, having loosed the pains of death, because it was not possible that He should be held by it.*" (brackets added).

In other words, Jesus could not be held in the grave because death was powerless to hold him. When up against Jesus, death is a wimp. It's feeble. It's got little spaghetti arms.

What does that mean for us?

It means, even if the worst-case scenario happens, we have nothing to fear. Even if it's death. Death was already defeated. That battle has been waged and won by Jesus on the cross. And that same power that raised Jesus from the dead now lives in us (Romans 8:11).

That's miracle-working power. It rids us of the torment we worry we'll never overcome. That's the power over mental anguish. That's the power for peace.

FEAR FROM THE START

Fear has been around awhile. The first instance, in fact, showed up in the Garden of Eden with Adam. Let's take a look at Genesis 3:1 to see how fear first entered mankind's storyline:

> *Now the serpent was more cunning than any beast of the field which the Lord God had made...*

It's creeping in already. Do you see it? Do you sense it? Isn't that just like fear to slither in like a snake?

> *...And he said to the woman, "Has God indeed said, 'You shall not eat of every tree of the garden?'"*

Let me set the stage here so you can really get the full weight of what's occurring. When God made Adam and Eve, He made them in His image for the specific job of subduing and taking authority over the birds, air, creatures, and ground. Anything that God made for or of the earth, Adam and Eve had dominion over it.

When God gave instructions about how to view and treat the trees in the Garden, Eve wasn't actually there. She got that knowledge second-hand from Adam. This is significant because of the great deception about to happen. Let's read on and see what vile plan the serpent had in mind.

> *And the woman said to the serpent, "We may eat the fruit of the trees of the garden; but of the fruit of the*

*tree which is in the midst of the garden, God has said,
'You shall not eat it, nor shall you touch it, lest you
die'"* (Genesis 3:2-3).

Right here, the woman has already erred. She misunderstood the directions. God never said they couldn't touch the fruit, only that they couldn't eat it. Because she didn't hear it directly from God, she took the information second-hand, added to it, and ended up with parts that weren't true.

That is one of the tricks of the enemy. He will take a little truth and twist it.

Once truth has been perverted, fear creeps in because even a little bit of untruth makes it not truth. It's either all or nothing with truth. Something is true. Or something is not. There are not degrees.

Okay, now back to the Garden.

*Then the serpent said to the woman, "You will not
surely die. For God knows that in the day you eat of
it your eyes will be opened, and you will be like God,
knowing good and evil"* (Genesis 3:4-5).

The father of lies sure came up with a couple of doozies!

Right now, I want to focus on one that rarely gets mentioned: Eve didn't need to be like God because she was already created in His image. She resembled her Father already. However, because she wasn't there from the beginning, she didn't have the same security with God that Adam had. See how crafty satan can be? He attacks our identity as children of God.

> ## EVE DIDN'T NEED TO BE LIKE GOD BECAUSE SHE WAS ALREADY CREATED IN HIS IMAGE.

Jesus, too, suffered this kind of attack. In Luke 4, when Jesus was tempted, satan made this statement to Jesus repeatedly, *"If You are the Son of God..."* He attacked Jesus' very identity.

THE JEALOUS SNAKE

We talked about Adam and Eve being created in God's image for a specific purpose: to have dominion over all the earth. That's what satan really wants. He tries to undermine our relationship with God and our identity as children of God so he can rob us of our power to use our authority.

Satan has no power over us. Jesus defeated him, praise God! So, the only card he has left to play against us is deception.

This is where the fear comes in. The devil wants to keep us distracted with our fears over what might happen so that we become powerless and self-destructive.

In reality, the devil can't stop us from doing anything. We blame him for a lot, but he doesn't have that kind of power anymore. If you are born again, if you are a believer in Jesus Christ, you have everything you need to succeed. You can do anything God calls you to do. Nothing is impossible for them who believe.

We can look to our perfect Savior and how the devil treated Him to know exactly what the devil is doing to us. He tempted Jesus with thoughts. He tried to plant seeds of doubt. What did he say? "If You really are the Son of God, then do this, do that..."

Jesus could have acted on those thoughts. He could have said to Himself, "I need to prove myself. I need to do something." But He didn't.

Today, satan is doing the same thing to us that he did to Jesus two thousand years ago. He's working day and night to deceive us. Before long, we're meditating on the wrong things and forgetting to use our own authority.

Let's be honest with ourselves here. Many times, we are our own worst enemy in the way we think. We obsess about the negative, create a cycle of anxiety, and then wonder why we're afraid.

Back in the Garden, Eve found herself led into that cycle by satan. He told her, "If you do this, then your eyes will be opened, and you'll be like God." She feared that she was missing out on something, that God was holding out on her. Because she did not understand she was already made in the image of God, she allowed satan to convince her to do something she never should have done to get something she already had.

GOD'S PRECIOUS PROMISES

You can look at this scenario in the context of healing or prosperity or other areas of lack in our lives, but what God is showing us is that Jesus has already deposited those things into our lives through the cross.

Because of Jesus' perfect sacrifice, we already have every good and precious promise. We already have everything we'll ever need to live successful, happy, healthy lives. If we've received Jesus in our hearts, then we're the carriers of the King of Glory. The Holy Spirit dwells inside us and we're blessed with every spiritual blessing in heavenly places (Ephesians 1:3).

In Colossians 2:9-10, we are told, *"For in Him dwells all the fullness of the Godhead bodily; and you are complete in Him, who is the head of all principality and power."* This is like saying, "God has already given us everything we need in our spirits to live a victorious life in this world."

This means that those circumstances that are stressing you out? Making you fear? You're already above them, not beneath them.

LEADING US INTO FEAR

Let's see how Eve responded to satan's lies:

> So when the woman saw that the tree was good for food,
> that it was pleasant to the eyes, and a tree desirable to
> make one wise, she took of its fruit and ate. She also
> gave to her husband with her, and he ate (Genesis 3:6).

This was the opportune time for Eve's husband to show
leadership. Adam could have been stern and called her out on
her disobedience. "No, Eve. Not that tree. Never that tree. We
will not do this." Or, he could have been sweeter and led by
being servant minded. "No thanks, babe. How about a peach
instead? I'll go pick one for you." Either one would have been a
better response than biting off a chunk of that forbidden fruit.

Whomever you are following, make sure they have truth on
their side. This is true in every situation, family life included. Truth
and peace flow from the top down, as does fear and torment.

If you've ever worked for a boss whose leadership style is
fear, you understand what I'm saying. *Their* fear will eventually
manifest in *your* mind and body.

FEAR'S CONSEQUENCES

For Adam and Eve, their lack of identity, poor leadership, and
underlying fear led them out of the Garden and permanently

separated them from God. The consequences of fear are always dreadful:

> *Then the eyes of both of them were opened, and they knew that they were naked; and they sewed fig leaves together and made themselves coverings. And they heard the sound of the Lord God walking in the garden in the cool of the day, and Adam and his wife hid themselves from the presence of the Lord God among the trees of the garden. Then the Lord God called to Adam and said to him, "Where are you?"* (Genesis 3:7-9).

Then, in verse 10, Adam, trembling and naked, responds, *"I heard Your voice in the garden, and was afraid."*

Here is the first instance of the word "afraid" in the Bible. Right here. They were afraid, due to their nakedness, so they hid. Their insecurity came directly from their lack of identity.

This can be true for us, too. When we don't understand who we are in Christ and the magnitude of what that means, when we don't fully recognize the person we are now or the power we now have in Jesus, we'll grow insecure. We'll feel guilty and sinful, and won't operate in the authority that is ours. Instead, we'll allow fear to creep in and separate us from God. He never leaves us—He never left Adam and Eve—but we'll fear our vulnerability.

The end result? We hold God, the very answer to our insecurity, at arm's length.

Like Adam, we'll resort to covering ourselves up and hiding things in our lives. Fear will lead us to shame, shame pushes us to hide, hiding separates us from others. And in the loneliness, torment rages.

OPEN HEARTS SING OPENLY

Have you ever noticed how children love to show off? They dance and sing and play, chanting "Look at me! Look! Look!" It doesn't even matter if they're any good, they love showing you what they can do. They live without fear of people.

However, as we get older, we allow fear to creep in from negative opinions and hurtful experiences. Soon, that childlike fearlessness is gone, replaced with adult-sized insecurity.

We absorb the natural fears, phobias, and insecurities of our environment. As we mature into adulthood, those fears we didn't have as children become very present. Like we were discussing earlier about the fear of public speaking, many adults who are traumatized by getting on that stage loved the spotlight as a small child.

As Christians, part of our new nature is to return to that childlike peace. God calls us to be bold and confident in Christ. When we allow that to come out, we show Jesus dwelling within us.

When my son, Joshua, was little he would make up songs. One day, we were in the supermarket with little Josh sitting in the cart as Ashley and I went about getting our groceries.

Though we'd never taught him any song of the kind, he started singing, "I'm so awesome. Yes, I am. Yes, I am!"

He sang with great confidence. Great, loud confidence. A confidence that started drawing the attention of other stoic, English shoppers.

Immediately, Ashley and my own insecurities crept up. *What would everyone think of our operatic little boy?* We tried to shush Josh but that just made him sing louder.

Looking back, Josh has never had an insecurity problem. I truly believe God was showing him, even at that young age, how He saw him: as Josh the Awesome. He knows who he is and doesn't fall victim to the enemy's lies. The kid is downright bold.

OUR HIGH PRIEST

When Adam heard the voice of God, he hid. Because of his fear. Because of his shame. He ran away from the very answer to his issue.

We often make the same mistake. By putting on a brave face or hiding our pain, we're sewing together pieces of fig leaves to cover our shame. We're putting on a mask and swatting away God's loving touch.

He is the healer of our hearts. We have to let Him work His perfect work, though. Keeping Him at a distance and refusing to deal with our fears will rob us of His comfort and deliverance.

Hebrews 4:15 tells us about who it is we're hiding from when we try to run away from confronting our fears: *"For we do not have a High Priest who cannot sympathize with our weaknesses, but was in all points tempted as we are, yet without sin."*

Don't let this slip by you. Jesus, too, was tempted with fear, tempted to question His identity. When satan challenged Him to prove He was the Son of God, Jesus faced that temptation. And overcame it.

Hebrews 4:16 continues, *"Let us therefore come boldly to the throne of grace, that we may obtain mercy and find grace to help in time of need."*

When we feel afraid, that's exactly when we need to run to God with more passion! To seek Him most earnestly. To reach out to Him, knowing without a doubt He's there.

When Adam sinned, he needed God in that moment more than ever. And God, the Father of grace and love, was there for him. God didn't hide from Adam and He'll never hide from us.

In times of fear and shame, satan may tell us to hide from God because we've messed up. He will try to convince us God won't be there for us. Remember, however, satan is the father of lies.

The truth is, there is no shame, guilt, or past mistake that should ever hold you back from God. He still wants a relationship with you. Always. It doesn't matter what you've done, what you've said, where you've been, who you've hurt, or how badly you've messed up.

When God looks at you, He sees His Son. He sees His image-bearer, whom He made in His image, with His authority, and with His power. He has a passionate plan for you that's good. So, throw yourself and all your fear, failings, and mental anguish on Him, the healer of your heart.

CHAPTER 4

HIS FEAR-BUSTING LOVE

DO YOU KNOW WHO YOU ARE?

Eve didn't know who she was. Not really. She doubted. Or, maybe she never fully comprehended. She had been placed in a position of authority alongside Adam to subdue all the earth, and she still thought she needed more.

She opened the door to fear because of her insecurity in her identity. If she'd only understood God's love for her. If she'd only been confident in that love. Perfect love casts out fear. That's what she could have been enjoying: fearless living. Instead, she doubted, fear entered, and sin followed close behind.

We've been studying her and Adam's fall from the Garden of Eden, which is accounted in Genesis 3. That is where we find the first instance of fear noted in the Bible.

Adam and Eve ate. They heard God's voice. And they were afraid. That fear begat shame, and that shame sent them hiding. Now seeing their nakedness, they scurried about to create poor substitutes to cover themselves.

Eve listened to the lies of the serpent as he questioned her identity, and this is where it led her.

Gone was that trust between her and God. Gone was the perfect communion. In its place, she had lies.

SATAN'S LIMITATIONS AND LEVERAGE

The enemy can't stop us from being born again. He can't stop us from receiving the promises of God. But if he can get us to question our relationship with God, we'll start operating in fear. When we don't understand our real identity as children of God, and the power that comes with that real identity, we give satan wiggle room to start whispering in our ears.

With Eve, he told her, "Just eat of this fruit and you'll be like God."

Without realizing she had already been created in God's image, she fell for that forked tongue. She focused more on the lies of the enemy than the promises of God and His Word. And the faith and confidence she had with God dissipated.

In the absence of that confidence, Eve feared. And that fear led to shame. And that shame led to separation from God. She not only welcomed fear, she gave away her authority.

MANKIND GETS HIRED

Adam and Eve had a job. They were commanded to go and subdue the animals of the earth, the birds of the air, and take dominion over all things on the earth. Eve took that authority, that power, that blessing, that inheritance, and gave it to the enemy. And that battle is still raging. That's why we have the lies and power of the enemy operating in the earth today.

But, there's good news!

When Jesus came, He died on the cross, rose again, and stripped the enemy of the power to harm us. He took back the keys of the kingdom. He restored mankind's power, authority, and identity.

Jesus changed everything. Because of Him, we don't have to live like orphan children. We can live like children of God. We've been adopted into His family with His power, His name, and His authority.

We can live fearlessly, which means being bold, brave, and intrepid. We don't have to fear anything in this world anymore because Jesus paid that price. There's nothing more we owe. In fact, fear isn't even part of who we are nor who we were created to be.

REVERENTIAL FEAR

When we're talking about fear, it's important to understand we're not referring to the fear of the Lord. That is completely different. That's reverence. It's an honoring fear. The fear of the Lord is referring to living our lives in awe and wonder of God's omnipotence.

Reverential fear is recognizing the bigness, the mightiness of God. It's looking to Him in amazement of who He is. That's a healthy fear. It's a fear that does not involve torment. It never holds you back. It never bears fruit of anxiety or anguish.

> # REVERENTIAL FEAR DOES NOT INVOLVE TORMENT. IT NEVER HOLDS YOU BACK. IT NEVER BEARS FRUIT OF ANXIETY OR ANGUISH.

It's the opposite.

I like how it's phrased in 1 John 4:4: *"You are of God, little children, and have overcome them, because He who is in you* [this is referring to the Holy Spirit] *is greater than he who is in the world"* (brackets added).

Through Jesus, we have overcome the world. In Christ, we are victorious. Romans 8:37 says, *"Yet in all these things we are more than conquerors through Him who loved us."*

The real you has overcome whatever trial is coming against you. You've already got that next big mountain in front of you climbed and conquered. Whatever you're worried about right now? Whatever is making you anxious? You've already won! Christ has already overcome it for you.

IN-CHRISTED

One of our ministry friends puts it this way, "You've been in-Christed."

When you said yes to Jesus, were born again, and made Him the Lord of your Life, you got in-Christed. And, now, in Christ, you're an overcomer. Whatever comes, God has given you the strength to overcome it. The ability is now with you. So, really, fear simply isn't who you are anymore.

Ephesians 1:4 says, *"He [Jesus] chose us in Him before the foundation of the world, to be holy and blameless before Him in love"* (MEV, brackets added).

Before God put the earth together—before He flowed the waters down the river beds, before He filled the oceans, before He stretched out the lands, before He oxygenated the air, before He placed the stars precisely where they could shine brightest and the moon could be most adored—God thought of you.

Before all of it, He had you in mind. He had your picture in His wallet.

He chose your hair color, eye color, your character and nature. He planned the days you'd be given. He mapped out all the wonderful places He wanted to take you and experiences He wanted to do with you.

Before God had a world for you to live in, He chose you to be with Him forever. Ephesians 1:5-6 says, *"He predestined us to adoption as sons to Himself through Jesus Christ according to the good pleasure of His will, to the praise and glory of His grace which He graciously bestowed on us in the Beloved"* (MEV).

God chose us to be in secure relationship with Him; He did not choose us to be fearful.

THE SLAVE MENTALITY

In the Old Testament, the children of God were persecuted, held captive, and used as slaves. In Exodus, we read about Moses freeing them from slavery and God moving them toward the Promised Land. As His children, God wanted to bless them by taking them to the land He had prepared for them.

However, even though they were free from slavery physically, they were still captives in their minds. It took them years to renew their minds and see themselves as God intended. We often experience the same in our lives today.

Galatians 5:1 says, *"For freedom Christ freed us."* Never again are we to be held captive. Yet, in our minds, fear can keep us in that slave mentality because we do not understand what it means to be adopted into His family.

When we consider that God planned us before the foundation of the world and chose us as His beloved, when we truly understand how much God loves us, that perfect love casts out our fear (1 John 4:18).

BEFORE ANY OF THIS...

Ashley had a moment when his adoption into God's family really hit home. I'll let him tell you about it:

> Here in Colorado Springs, we have a park called Garden of the Gods. Formed thousands of years ago, this park winds around these rocks the size of high-rise buildings. It's incredible.
>
> One day, I was driving around the Garden of the Gods, marveling at the rock formations, and the Lord spoke to me saying, "Before any of this came about..." He was reminding me He was aware of me and my life and my future before any of these rocks had even been formed.
>
> It's a good reminder for all of us. Wherever you are in the world, look around your environment. Look at the mountains or the sea or the natural landscape and consider that God had you in mind, had a plan for you, and had chosen you before He created anything you're seeing.
>
> God didn't create us and leave us to our own devices. Right from the start, when Adam and Eve gave over their authority, God put a plan in place to

redeem us back to Himself. He did it all because of His love for us and His desire for an intimate relationship with us. We are His temple, a place where God dwells.

Well, if I'm like this and like that, God will love me more, we often think. But that is not God's unconditional love. We can do nothing to hinder God's love or to make Him love us more. He does not love you because of who you are but because of who He is.

That kind of love changes things. It gives us security and casts out fear.

When we can accept a Father's love that never leaves or forsakes us, we stop wondering if God will protect us, provide for us, heal us, fix us. We stop wondering if God has good plans for our lives.

In the love of God, there is protection and provision. That's faith. It's trusting in the Word of God more than the lies of the enemy. And that faith gives us access to the promises of God.

KNOCK, KNOCK

I remember the moment I first got a glimpse of how much God loved me. I was at home getting my praise on in the kitchen. Suddenly, there was a knock at the door.

I was home alone with our three kids—a newborn, a one-year-old, and a two-year-old—at that time.

When I turned the latch on the door, it was immediately forced open. A large man, a stranger, was trying to force his way into the house. He was shouting and swearing and aggressively entering our home, while yelling that I had his money.

He was some kind of debt collector and convinced I owed him. If he didn't get his money, he threatened to hurt me, hurt my children, and burn our house down. It was horrific.

As the backstory started to unfold, I learned he worked for some local loan shark. We had recently had to fire an employee who stole a car from us. This employee had gotten into trouble with the loan shark. When he got caught unable to pay, he gave the loan shark our address and said, "These people have got your money. Go collect it."

This guy showed up at our front door ready to collect.

With Ashley at work, the mama bear in me came out with a roar.

"Oh no, buster," I told him, "You're not going to come in here."

All five feet of me rose up to meet this challenge. Whoever this man was, whoever he worked for, however he thought he could threaten me, I wasn't going to have it!

What came out of me at that moment of faith was fearlessness. I had every reason to fear, but I didn't. The enemy had attacked me during a moment when I'd been completely lost in the delight of God's presence. With God, there is never any reason to fear. His love is a powerful force of protection. In that realm, fear has no place.

So, I looked this uncircumcised Philistine in the eyes, pointed my finger at his nose, and said, "Who do you think you are coming at me? What right do you have coming around to collect money from me?"

> GOD'S LOVE IS A POWERFUL FORCE OF PROTECTION. IN THAT REALM, FEAR HAS NO PLACE.

He was coming against the armies of the living God! I have a covenant with the Lord Almighty. He had no rights there, so I came at him in faith. Every word that came out of my mouth was like swinging a punch. They were words of power. And, even though I never touched him, I could see the fear of the Lord in his eyes.

Slowly, he staggered backward down the garden path. When he reached the fence post, he held on as if trying to steady himself. After one last look back, he took off running down the road. When he looked back at me in that moment, it was like he saw something else. I believe it was the supernatural protection of God. He was seeing those angels encamping around me from Psalm 91.

CHOOSING AND RECEIVING LOVE

We experience the true power of faith when we keep ourselves in the love of God. His love for us is always constant, always there, always on, always available. But we have to choose to accept it.

In the writings of John, he described himself as the disciple whom Jesus loved. He was the one who rested his head on Jesus' chest and also ran to him when he saw Him in the distance.

Jesus didn't love John any more than the other disciples, but John understood the extent of Jesus' love for him more fully. It gave him boldness to rest lovingly against Him at dinner, to seek that intimate connection, to be vulnerable with his Savior.

When Jesus was being crucified, there was only one disciple who was fearless enough to stand at the foot of the cross. What made John different from the others? He knew he was loved, and it cast out all the naturally occurring fear of that horrific day.

There is nothing you can do to make God love you more. As my husband and I often say, grace has already done it. That work is complete. God has made up His mind about His love for you and it's constant and forever.

However, we must choose to receive God's love and there are steps we can take to do that.

I like how Jude puts it: *"But you, beloved, build yourselves up in your most holy faith"* (Jude 20 MEV).

Before we go any further, I want to land on the word "beloved" for a moment. In Scripture, Jesus was called the "beloved" Son of God about seven times. God said, "This is My beloved Son, in whom I am well pleased."

So, that's where we start: accepting that we are loved.

Jude 21 says, *"Keep yourselves in the love of God, looking for the mercy of our Lord Jesus Christ unto eternal life."*

That is a key to overcoming fear. When you meditate on how much God loves you and how much He's already done for you, that eradicates a lot of the fear plaguing your life. It flips a light on and burns away all the shadows surrounding the unknown.

Jeremiah 29:11 can be that light switch. Here is a paraphrase taken from multiple versions of the Bible: "For I know the thoughts I think toward you, the plans I have toward you, says the Lord. Thoughts to prosper you, thoughts to increase you, thoughts to give you an expected end, a hope and a future."

Those are God's thoughts toward you. If that's where we direct our minds, we'll find our fears begin to shrink under the power of God's love.

Above all, we want to keep our minds stayed on God like Isaiah 26:3 instructs, *"You will keep him in perfect peace, whose mind is stayed on You, because he trusts in You."*

GIFT YOUR FEAR TO GOD

A big part of overcoming fear is recognizing it's there, it's real, and you can trust God with it. But, how? That's the big issue. We want to trust God with our fear, but we're at a loss to know how to let it go and give it to Him.

I had the same problem. Over the years, I've dealt with a lot of fear. Some of it came from events in my childhood. Some fears were rational. Some were based in trauma. All needed to be handed over to God for me to live fearlessly.

To better do this, God gave me a visual representation. When God told me to take every fearful thought captive (2 Corinthians 10:5), He knew I needed a mental picture to take me through the process.

Start by imagining a box, like a shoe box, a hat box, a Tiffany Blue Box. Feel free to get creative. Make it real for you.

Then, take that ugly fear (feel free to imagine using gloves here when touching it) and shove that Philistine into the box. Slam the lid down tight! Tape it closed, if you like. If it's a plain box, pull out the mental wrapping paper. Wrap it and bind it and slap a bow on top. Make it look like a gift.

When you're all done, place that box into the hands of God and leave it with Him.

Psalm 55:22 says, *"Cast your burden on the Lord, and He shall sustain you."* He is the only One who can handle the ugliness inside that box. In fact, He's already defeated that fear on the cross. It's done.

When you hand over that fear, tell Him, "Lord, I see this is a fear. I see this is a lie. I'm going to give it to You, and I'm not going to take it back. I'm going to entrust it with You."

Anytime that fear comes again, I tell it, "Return to sender." I'm not taking that fear back.

CAST FEAR DOWN

Fear has a huge ego. Did you know that? It's a lie that exalts itself above the knowledge of God.

Fear counters the truth by telling us, "This isn't going to work out," or, "This (insert bad thing) is going to happen to you."

In 2 Corinthians 10:4-5, we can see the battle clearly. It says, *"For the weapons of our warfare are not carnal but mighty in God for pulling down strongholds, casting down arguments and every high thing that exalts itself against the knowledge of God."*

That stronghold, that repeating fear habit we can't seem to conquer, must be cast down. You have to bring those thoughts into captivity and make them obedient to Jesus.

If you're wondering whether or not you're battling a stronghold, give it the John 10:10 test. Are these thoughts you're having coming to kill, steal, and destroy? Or do they give you life and life more abundantly?

In Philippians 4:8, we see the things we're instructed to meditate on: things that are true, that are right, that are pure, that are lovely, that are praiseworthy—that is where we must direct our minds. When we do, when we turn away from the negative thoughts, we're casting them away from us and giving them to God.

HOLY SPIRIT POWER

If we want to live a fearless life, we must have the power of the Holy Spirit. That is where we're going to find our boldness and our strength to cast down any strongholds.

Now, I want to be clear here. You can be born again and not baptized in the Holy Spirit. You're still going to Heaven, God still loves you, but you're missing out on blessings God has for you.

The baptism of the Holy Spirit is a separate experience from salvation.

When you received Jesus, you received the Holy Spirit. However, when you experience the baptism of the Holy Spirit, you activate the power of God dwelling inside you.

In the first chapter of Acts, Jesus instructed His disciples to wait in the upper room until the Holy Spirit came upon them. Even Jesus Himself was baptized in the Holy Spirit before He performed any miracles.

Afterward, you can see the difference the Holy Spirit made in the lives of the disciples. It was especially evident in the life of Peter. Before the Holy Spirit, Peter allowed fear to cause him to deny Jesus three times. After the Holy Spirit, Peter preached boldly and three thousand people were saved. Powered by the Holy Spirit, Peter dedicated his life to preaching the Gospel in the face of very real fears, including his own death.

Now *that's* power.

POWER IN THE TONGUE

One of the many benefits of the baptism of the Holy Spirit is a prayer language. Through the Holy Spirit, you can pray in tongues. This is a powerful tool that may frighten some. It did me, initially, due to my own church background and misunderstanding about the whole tongues business.

However, as I recognized it as a gift from God, I began to desire every good and precious gift He offers. I received that gift and, now, if I struggle with fear, I find power to overcome by praying in tongues.

When we're praying in the Spirit, we can pray for the perfect will of God. Sometimes, when we're overcome with fear, we don't know how or even what to pray. That's when we can pray in tongues. This allows us to focus our minds and keep our thoughts upon God.

We looked at the first half of Jude 20 a moment ago, but the complete verse reads, *"But you, beloved, build yourselves up in your most holy faith. Pray in the Holy Spirit"* (MEV).

Jude instructs us to build ourselves up by praying in the Holy Spirit. One way we keep ourselves in the love of God, which is our weapon against fear, is our prayer language. When we pray in the Holy Spirit, in our prayer language, we keep ourselves in the love of God.

Paul, in his writing to Jude, is giving a practical tool on how to keep ourselves in the love of God. We pray in the Holy Spirit, which keeps our mind on God, which keeps us in the love of God.

As you pray in tongues, even though you're not praying in your native language, your mind is receiving wisdom and revelation from God. You cannot operate in fear and pray in tongues at the same time. It's such a powerful tool in battling against fear; I hope you will be encouraged to seek it out!

CHAPTER 5

FEAR AND UNBELIEF: BEST BUDDIES

IS THE DEVIL REAL?

One night when our daughter Hannah was four, we were explaining to her the difference between something real and something fake. We would ask her about this, ask her about that, and she'd tell us if it was real or fake.

Apples: real. Mermaids: fake. And so on.

Then Ashley gave her a trick question. He asked, "Is the devil real or fake?"

I still remember her looking out the window, while her little mind worked through the question. She finally said, "Dad, the devil is real, but his weapons are fake."

That was a clearer revelation than many adults in the body of Christ have about the devil. He is real, but his weapons are fake!

THE DEVIL IS REAL, BUT HIS WEAPONS ARE FAKE.

HE LOST AND HE KNOWS IT

As I mentioned before, the number one fake weapon the devil uses is deception. That's his go-to tool. His favorite gun. His sharpest knife. His skill in its use is unsurpassed. However, because of Jesus, it's useless against us when we recognize *who we are!*

The devil is afraid of the children of God because he's already been defeated by our Father. He has no authority over us, no power. The only thing he can do is bomb us with lies and hope we allow one to detonate.

Our authority in Jesus terrifies him. When we understand what Jesus has done, what He accomplished on that cross, we become deadly to satan's schemes. We know the truth and the truth defeats deception every time.

DEAD TO DECEPTION

When we start seeing through the devil's lies, he can't trick us anymore. Lies don't work. Deception fails. And satan fears.

He knows we have authority over him. The only thing he has over us is deception and, when it fails, so does he.

In chapter four, we talked about how fear has no part in who we are as born-again believers. God has not given us the spirit of fear, but of power, love, and a sound mind (2 Timothy 1:7). He has placed His very nature, His character, into us through the fruit of the spirit: love, joy, peace, patience, kindness, goodness, faithfulness, gentleness, self-control. All those godly attributes are mentioned in Galatians 5:22-23, and fear isn't mentioned once.

It's simply not who we are.

God did not design us to be in fear. Once we start to understand who God created us to be, we become deadly to the plans of the enemy. Our security in Christ stops us from handing the devil our authority. Instead, like Romans 8 shows, we become more than conquerors.

A FEARLESS INHERITANCE

In Romans 8:14, it says, *"For as many as are led by the Spirit of God, these are sons of God."* If you've given your life to Jesus, you are a son or daughter of God. In verse 15, it tells us that as His child we do *"not receive the spirit of bondage again to fear."*

Instead of the spirit of fear, we're given *"the spirit of adoption."* This means we can rightly call upon God as "Abba, Father," which is like saying, "Daddy God." It's personal and very paternal.

In this adoption, we learn, *"The Spirit Himself bears witness with our spirit that we are children of God, and if children, then heirs—heirs of God and joint heirs with Christ"* (Romans 8:16-17).

This is a powerful statement. It means everything Jesus gained at the cross is now ours when we're born again. Like I mentioned previously, we were in-Christed. We are now in Christ and He lives in us, which means living with peace, with faith, and without fear.

We are joint heirs with Christ, which is such an amazing blessing it deserves a "Praise God!"

When we skip down to Romans 8:37, it says we are *"more than conquerors through Him who loved us."* Through our relationship with Jesus, we reap the spoils of the price He paid. We gave Him our pain, suffering, sin, and fear, and He went to the cross for us and exchanged it all for His righteousness, health, healing, peace of mind, and faith.

This is why the Gospel message is so overwhelming. When we start to understand what God has done for us through Jesus, it almost seems too good to be true!

TESTING FOR FEAR

How do we know when we're in fear or in faith? That might seem like a strange question, but it's one I get asked frequently because fear can often be quite subtle and downright sneaky.

For example, someone may come forward for healing. They say they're believing in faith. However, when you listen to their prayers, they're actually full of fear. They're praying frantically. These aren't faith-filled prayers, they are fear-filled. They're crying out to God in crisis-driven prayers.

One of the characteristics of faith, however, is peace. If we do not have peace, then our prayers are coming from a place of fear. Our motivation is fear.

JESUS CONFRONTS FEAR

Instead of being driven by fear, I want you to receive everything God has for you. To understand the difference between praying in faith and praying in fear, let's look at how Jesus identified fear and overcame it.

In Luke 8:49, we meet Jairus, who is also mentioned in Matthew 9 and Mark 5. *"While He [Jesus] was still speaking, someone came from the ruler of the synagogue's house, saying to him [Jairus], 'Your daughter is dead. Do not trouble the Teacher'"* (brackets added for clarity).

Jesus was actually on His way to Jairus' house. Jairus had asked Jesus to come and lay hands on his sick daughter. So, the Savior was on His way, but got delayed. On the journey there, He met a woman with an issue of blood.

Now, if I'm Jairus, I'm standing there thinking, *Come on! My daughter doesn't have much time!* I would understand that this woman needed help, too, but we're talking about my baby girl here. She's at home dying! I would be getting impatient, getting frustrated, trying to hurry Jesus up.

Jesus, however, never panics. Not when a man was filled with a legion of demons, or when Lazarus' friends urged Him to hurry before it was too late, or when his disciples were sure they were going to die in a boat-sinking storm.

Jesus was never affected by any crisis. Instead, He always remained calm. His will is to bring healing, but He didn't run frantically into those situations. He operated in consistent peace because Jesus knew His authority.

He also knew how it would all end. He knew, even if Jairus' daughter died, He could raise her from the dead.

Then the report came. Jairus' daughter had died. This man received the worst news of his life. His nightmare had become a reality. Jesus delayed, and his baby girl was gone.

I haven't been through the exact same situation, but I have been given the report by doctors to take my daughter home to die. That kind of news moves you at a heart level. I don't care how spiritual you are, you would battle to stay in a place of peace hearing a report like that.

However, just like our daughter's story, Jairus' daughter's story is a good one, too.

In verse 50, Jesus heard the report and answered, *"Do not be afraid; only believe and she will be made well."* The same moment is captured in Mark 5:36 as, *"Overhearing but ignoring what they said, Jesus said to the ruler of the synagogue, Do not be seized with alarm and struck with fear; only keep on believing"* (AMPC).

FEAR'S STOPPING POWER

Jesus hears a fearful report and tells everyone to keep on believing. Don't be seized with alarm. Don't be paralyzed by fear. Keep on believing. He's addressing the effects He knows fear can have on our mortal hearts.

In the Old Testament, we see that paralyzing nature of fear in the story of Lot and his wife. As they were escaping Sodom and Gomorrah, they were told not to look back. But Lot's wife looked. She saw the destruction of the city and was turned into a pillar of salt.

Now, I'm not suggesting this could happen to you, but fear does paralyze.

Ashley experienced paralyzing fear firsthand during a frightening moment a few years back. Here's his harrowing tale:

> Years ago, I was out late and happened to drive past the church where I was currently employed. When I glanced over, I noticed the front door was wide open. It was about 11 o'clock at night. No one was working at that hour. So, everything should have been locked up tight.
>
> I took a deep breath and pulled into the parking lot. If someone had broken in, I needed to find out.

Inside, the church opened to a vast auditorium. A vast, dark auditorium. The light switch was on the other side of that pitch-black room. To get there, I had to walk across the auditorium without a flashlight, all while knowing someone could attack at any moment.

As I'm making my way across the auditorium, keeping my head swiveling and my eyes searching the shadows for movement, I noticed the pastor's office door was also ajar. And there, behind the door, was the shadow of a man.

Let me tell you, in that moment, I couldn't move. Suddenly, my brain went into a tailspin. What should I do? Should I rush through the door? Run away? Confront whoever lurked behind the door? Get out of there and call the police?

It felt like I stood there deliberating for an eternity, but it was probably only thirty seconds. A long thirty seconds. All of which I stood there without being able to take a single step forward or backward.

In the back of my mind, I could see all the nightmare scenarios playing out. The person behind that door could be dangerous. He could have a gun. He could attack. This might be the last few seconds before my life changed forever, or even ended.

I had no idea what awaited me in that next minute. The threat. The unknowns. I couldn't see past them to make a decision.

Finally, the adrenaline kicked in, and I burst forward. I yanked the door completely open to tackle the man and, instead, tackled a robe.

Yeah, it was a robe.

I don't know what it says about me that I saw my life flash before my eyes because of a church door that was poorly latched and a vicar's robe, but I experienced how immobilizing fear can be.

SEIZED WITH ALARM

Fear not only torments our minds, but it also affects our physical bodies. Adrenaline kicks in and, suddenly, we're crazed with that fight or flight impluse.

Once fear takes over, our bodies stop responding to our commands and, instead, respond to our fear. I've seen people scared of heights, for instance, who lock up the moment they're faced with that fear.

Jesus addressed this response when Jairus received his heartbreaking news. He didn't breeze past it or brush it aside. He gave specific instruction on how we should respond to that panic when it wells up inside us.

Let's look at Luke 8:50 again to explain: *"Do not be afraid; only believe, and she will be made well."*

The tense this was written in is called the present, imperative tense. It means a continuous action or command. In other words, Jesus wasn't simply saying, "Oh, there, there Jairus. Don't worry. It's going to be okay." What Jesus was actually saying was, "No! Don't you fear. Don't you do it. Don't give it one inch. Stop it right now, and never do it again."

He spoke forcefully and bluntly to Jairus because He knew this father was in the middle of the war between faith and fear at that very moment. He was stopping Jairus from ever planting that seed of fear.

BELIEF IN THE NEGATIVE

Why is unbelief so detrimental? Because unbelief is basically belief in the negative.

Unbelief is based in fear. If we don't check our fear, if we don't contain it, if we don't go to war against it, that fear will result in unbelief. And that unbelief will hinder us from receiving everything God has for us.

We won't be able to operate in the spiritual gifts. We won't hear God's voice. We will doubt His love. And, like Eve, we'll hand over our authority to the enemy.

That is why Jesus was so pointed in stopping Jairus' fear before it could get a foothold. Jesus was stern out of His love for this grieving father.

It's that same love He has for us, too, and that same passion He has against our fear. He has many blessings and gifts prepared for us, and He doesn't want us to miss out on any of them.

SHUT UNBELIEF OUT

On the journey to Jairus' house, Jesus tells him not to be afraid but believe. Now, they've arrived at his home, and the daughter who has recently passed is inside.

In Luke 8:51, it says, *"When He came into the house, He permitted no one to go in except Peter, James, and John, and the father and mother of the girl."*

Scripture says He shut everyone else out. All these people were mourning, but He shut them out. You'd think He'd want to minister to everyone, right? Instead, He kept them outside. He was focused. He was there to bring a young girl back to life, and He knew how toxic fear can be.

Inside that home, Jesus knew there wasn't enough room for both fear *and* a miracle.

We can also frequently find ourselves in environments of fear. We may not even fear initially, but when we're around others who are fearful, eventually that fear can take root in us, too. Their reactions, their grief, their pain—we can start carrying that weight with us.

At Jairus' house, Jesus wasn't being insensitive to the feelings of the others. He wasn't being uncaring or uncompassionate.

He was giving them a different perspective on death and shutting the door to unbelief.

In another situation, Jesus took a blind man outside of town before praying for him (Mark 8:22-25). He walked him to the outskirts because that town was so writhing with unbelief. Unbelief was everywhere. That town reeked with the stench of it. Jesus said His mighty works there were of no effect because of that unbelief (Matthew 11:21).

JESUS KNEW THERE WASN'T ENOUGH ROOM FOR BOTH FEAR *AND* A MIRACLE.

We can shut the door to unbelief. We can throw it out of town. We can hit fear head on and stop it in its tracks.

Jesus accomplished this by removing fearful people from the environment and stopping them from entering. He created an atmosphere of faith.

FEAR AND THE FIVE SENSES

"All wept and mourned for the girl," Luke 8:52 tells us. The people were distraught, wailing and grieving and carrying on, completely overcome with the circumstances.

One of the characteristics of fear is that it focuses on the five senses: what it can see, smell, taste, touch, and hear. It considers only what's happening in the here and now, only the natural things.

Faith does the opposite. It goes beyond the five senses and operates in the spiritual realm. Hebrews 11:1 describes faith as being, *"the substance of things hoped for, the evidence of things not seen."*

Jesus looked beyond the five senses, beyond the natural realm. He knew the girl was dead. He saw the mourning. But He viewed the situation through eyes of faith.

By emulating Jesus, we can see beyond our fearful, natural circumstances and live in a place of belief where we can receive what God has for us. Like the blind man in the unbelieving city, Jesus led him beyond that environment and that's where he received his sight.

GO BEYOND THE TEMPORARY

Fear will always highlight what is naturally lacking in us. Whatever it is, whatever resource we lack, that's where fear will shine its spotlight because fear can only operate in what it sees.

But faith goes beyond that. It enters the supernatural where God's abilities and God's resources operate and are available. While fear only sees the temporary, faith sees the eternal.

When you're facing a fear, here's something that will help you see past the natural. Get right into that fear's face, toe to toe, nose to nose, and shout, "You're temporary!"

One of fear's biggest weak points is that it's subject to the natural world and, therefore, subject to change. Remind that fear who it is. And you will start to remember who you are in Christ.

In Luke 8:53, it says the people laughed at Jesus. In the verse prior, He had told them not to weep. *"She is not dead, but sleeping."* He came face to face with their fear and, instead of believing, they clung to their natural realm and laughed.

So, He shut that unbelief outside. And that's when the miracle happened. *"But He put them all outside, took her by the hand and called, saying, 'Little girl, arise.' Then her spirit returned, and she arose immediately"* (Luke 8:54-55).

Not mockery, not unbelief, not even death could stop the Son of God. Goodbye death. Hello life.

HOW TO SHUT OUT UNBELIEF

You want to do this. I know you do. You want to take your unbelief, march it outside your house, slam that door, and slide the deadbolt. You want to live in faith, but how is that possible?

I. RECOGNIZE THE CONNECTION

We must recognize the relationship between fear and unbelief. They're buddies. They're friends. They never go anywhere without the other. If you have one, you certainly are struggling with the other. So, see them for what they are: your enemies working together against you.

2. DOUBT THE CIRCUMSTANCES

You need to stop doubting God and start doubting your circumstances. Unbelief seeps in when we've bought more into satan's lies than we have the truth of God's Word.

3. NOTICE YOUR SENSES

Consider how much of your fear is based on what you're experiencing with your five senses. You may be living in uncertain circumstances, but circumstances change.

In 2 Corinthians 4:17, Paul describes his troubles as "light afflictions," even though Paul's afflictions weren't particularly light! They included everything from being shipwrecked, to being jailed, to beatings, and yet he called them light because they were *working for us a far more exceeding and eternal weight of glory.*

He saw beyond the natural realm to the spiritual, faith-filled one.

4. SHUT DOWN LIES

Rebuke the lies that are creating those moments of panic, anxiety, and torment. When we respond to our circumstances, our body responds with reactions all its own. We think we're reacting to what we're sensing, but fear clouds our perception. In reality, we may be physically reacting to something that isn't even true.

5. CONSIDER THE UNSEEN

Like the Apostle Paul, look to the things that are not seen. In 2 Corinthians 4:18, he says, *"We do not look at the things which are seen, but at the things which are not seen. For the things which are seen are temporary, but the things which are not seen are eternal."*

The things you are seeing (or feeling, tasting, hearing, smelling) are temporary, but the things you do not see are eternal. When compared to what the Lord says through His Word about who we are in Christ, everything else is but a vapor. Whether it's a sickness, a lack, an addiction, or a heartbreak— all are temporary.

THE EVIL OF UNBELIEF

As born-again believers, fear is no longer part of our nature. We shouldn't tolerate it. We shouldn't learn to live with it. It is not our normal. Fear, once allowed, leads to unbelief and hinders us from receiving everything God paid for.

Hebrews 3:12 tells us, *"Be attentive, brothers, lest there be in any of you an evil, unbelieving heart, and you depart from the living God"* (MEV).

In this verse, God is connecting evil with unbelief. Let's not miss the significance of this!

God understands sin is harmful to us, and He understands unbelief is harmful to us. He is warning us that an unbelieving heart will cause us to depart from the living God. When moving away from God, we will move toward lies.

When God led the children of Israel to the Promised Land, spies were sent in to survey the area and report back. In Numbers 13:1-14:10, we read about the spies being dispatched and then returning.

During their investigative mission, they took note of the giants in the land. Upon returning, instead of trusting God, all but Caleb and Joshua warned their people of all the dangers. These men only looked at the circumstances, instead of looking to the strength, power, and promises from God. And God called it an "evil report" (Numbers 13:32).

Remember, these are the people who had beheld the miracles of God with their own eyes. They witnessed the plagues. They walked on dry ground through the Red Sea. They were walking with God right beside them and, as soon as a few giants showed up, it was, "Thanks, but no thanks."

DON'T MISS OUT

We do this, too. God works miracles and blessings in our lives. He walks with us. He comforts us. He actively participates in our needs. Then, fear arises, and we forget it all. Instead, we focus only on what's wrong, on the threat, and we miss out on what God planned.

For the children of Israel, their fear of the giants hardened their hearts and they actually became disobedient. Because of their unbelief, God sent them into the wilderness for forty years until the bodies of that faithless generation were buried.

Instead of seeing the Promised Land, they lived the rest of their days in the desert. Instead of living with rich soil, soft grass, and cooling shade, they walked the burning sands.

They died in that wilderness, never beholding that Promised Land, because of their unbelief.

We don't want to miss out on anything God has for us due to unchecked fear. Jesus was quick to call out fear and stop it immediately. That's the example for us, too. To stop fear, we have to first see it, confront it, and allow Jesus to lead us to victory over it.

CHAPTER 6

THE REARVIEW MIRROR OF FEAR

DO YOU BELIEVE GOD LOVES YOU?

When we understand God's perfect love for us, there is no room for fear (1 John 4:18). His love is that powerful, which is why our understanding of it is that vital. Once we fully comprehend the height and depth and width and breadth of His love, we'll discover the security we so desperately need to finally overcome our fears.

Here's how 1 Peter 5:7 explains it, *"Casting all your care upon Him, for He cares for you."* God's care is so total, so complete, He willingly sacrificed His Son for us. In John 3:16, we learn that *"God so loved the world that He gave His only begotten Son."*

That's a love beyond anything here on Earth. It's love, plus.

THE NOISY CAT

In the next verse, in 1 Peter 5:8, we're forewarned about our number one enemy. *"Be sober, be vigilant; because your adversary the devil walks about like a roaring lion, seeking whom he may devour."*

Jesus defeated the devil on the cross. He took away his weapons, his authority, and you might say He knocked satan's teeth out. Notice the scripture says, *"whom he may devour."* It appears the devil *cannot* kill, steal, and destroy without permission!

So, what do you do? Take yourself off the devil's menu.

TAKE YOURSELF OFF THE DEVIL'S MENU.

When he asks to devour you, you deny him that liberty by not:

- listening to his lies.
- meditating on circumstances that generate fear.
- entertaining fear.
- accepting a state of living in fear.

Instead, you spot the fear instantly for what it is—a lie. Remember, FEAR is False Evidence Appearing Real. It's a perception of failure or defeat, sickness or poverty. It is not who we are. God created us to be victorious, successful, healthy, happy, prosperous people.

VICTORY OF THE MIND

To live fearlessly, we must take every thought captive. And we do so from the very beginning. Don't let your fearful thoughts get a foothold. Don't let them even leave a footprint behind.

Let's look at 1 Peter 5:7 in the Amplified Bible, Classic Edition to expound on this: *"Casting the whole of your care [all your anxieties, all your worries, all your concerns, once and for all] on Him, for He cares for you affectionately and cares about you watchfully."*

This is an intimate caring. He does not care for us out of obligation but out of sincere desire.

Oftentimes, we have a tendency to look at God's love as a responsibility. "Well, God has to care for me. I mean, He's God and we're His children. He has to care."

Scripture tells us differently. It says He cares affectionately, watchfully, proactively. He isn't waiting for us to get into trouble before He takes notice. He's looking ahead. He's warning us of dangers coming. Through His Holy Spirit, He's preparing us in order to protect us.

OUR FELLOW WARRIORS

Verses eight and nine continue, *"Be well balanced (temperate, sober of mind), be vigilant and cautious at all times; for that enemy of yours, the devil, roams around like a lion roaring [in fierce hunger], seeking someone to seize upon and devour. Withstand him; be firm in faith [against his onset—rooted, established, strong, immovable, and determined]..."*

We must be rooted, strong, immovable, and determined, but we don't get there on our own. God has already given us all the tools we need to resist the devil and his lies.

When he shows up, we can be ready for him.

Finishing up verse nine, it says, *"...knowing that the same (identical) sufferings are appointed to your brotherhood (the whole body of Christians) throughout the world."*

You're not alone in this. Whatever it is you fear, your fellow brothers and sisters in Christ are fighting, too.

As we've previously discussed, Jesus is our High Priest who knows our sufferings. He was tempted in every way like us but without committing sin (Hebrews 4:15). So, whatever we're struggling to overcome, He went through it. And not only Him. Our fellow brothers and sisters around the world have similar struggles warring against them.

This is important to remember because fear often brings with it a feeling of isolation. We may be worrying that we're not going to make it, things won't work out, and that our fears will become reality. And that this is our struggle alone. But, it's not. These are the devil's tricks, and he uses them liberally on everyone.

The truth is, the devil isn't all that creative.

KEEP LOOKING STRAIGHT AHEAD

One of the characteristics of fear is that it can only look backward. It's the only view it can access because it's the only view the devil can access. He can't see our future. He can only see our past.

Because he's been observing human nature for such a long time, he knows how to push our hot buttons. He knows what types of fear to use to their maximum benefit and what types of struggles create the biggest feelings of defeat. He looks at our past negative experiences and pushes those into the forefront of our minds until we believe our past will repeat itself in our future.

That's a lie.

While fear looks in the rearview mirror, faith is looking out the windshield at the open road ahead. It sees the possibilities. When fear says, "I see what's going on here and it's going to turn out exactly like last time," faith says, "I see what's going on here, *but* God's bigger than that."

Faith changes our perception. It takes our fear and our past experiences and paints a hopeful, optimistic, life-giving picture of our future. It alters how we see our challenges and gives us a vision of overcoming.

> # WHILE FEAR LOOKS IN THE REARVIEW MIRROR, FAITH IS LOOKING OUT THE WINDSHIELD AT THE OPEN ROAD AHEAD.

This hope then becomes rooted in our hearts. In Proverbs 23:7 it says that as a man thinks in his heart, so is he. If we perceive ourselves as victims, we'll be victim minded. If we perceive ourselves as victorious, despite the challenges we're facing, we'll be victorious.

SPY OUT THE CHALLENGES

We mentioned previously the spies in the land of Canaan. Let's dive a little deeper into the fear vs. faith aspects of this event.

Numbers 13:1-2 says, *"And the Lord spoke to Moses, saying, 'Send men to spy out the land of Canaan, which I am giving to the children of Israel; from each tribe of their fathers you shall send a man.'"*

God had given them the land. It was theirs for the taking! The next step was for Moses to send in the spies and everyone else to start packing their bags. They were headed to the Promised Land.

Further into the chapter, we learn the instructions Moses gave the men he had chosen:

> [Go] *and see what the land is like: whether the people who dwell in it are strong or weak, few or many; whether the land they dwell in is good or bad; whether the cities they inhabit are like camps or strongholds; whether the land is rich or poor; and whether there are forests there or not. Be of good courage* (Numbers 13:18, brackets added).

Moses, directed by God, was telling them to scope out the details. Come back with a report to inform Israel what was ahead and do it all courageously.

The spies entered the land on a reconnaissance mission. It wasn't time to take the land, only start strategizing how. But what they saw caused them to doubt and panic because they'd forgotten about all the miracles God had worked on their behalf. God had been with them, provided for them, defeated armies for them, but they were focused on their circumstances, instead.

When the spies returned, only two gave a positive report. Only two kept their eyes off their own perception and onto the power of God.

DRIVING WITHOUT A SEAT BELT

Like those faithless spies, a skewed perception can happen to us even in everyday life situations. It happened to Ashley when it came to a certain beach buggy and a certain wife driving it. He tells it so much better, so here's Ashley's freak out story:

> Years ago, I had a beach buggy that wasn't Carlie's favorite hobby of mine. It was a fixer-upper project and not what you might call the safest vehicle on the road. Although it was road legal, it probably wasn't road advised.
>
> Concerned, Carlie asked me if it was safe. And I assured her, "It's perfectly safe. Like a Volvo. You don't need to worry."
>
> The issue was…there weren't even seat belts in this vehicle. I rarely drove it on the road. Mostly, I was tinkering with it parked, but when I did drive it, I didn't want her to worry. So, when she pointed out the missing seat belts, I told her, "But, you know what? It has a roll cage. So, if I roll it, no biggie. I just keep my arms inside and I'm absolutely fine."
>
> It wasn't perfectly safe, actually. I never would have allowed anyone I love to ride in it. Carlie, however, didn't know that. So, one day while I was at a friend's house, she and some girlfriends took it for a spin.

When I called her phone, she didn't answer. Finally, I got through to a friend who knew where she was. He said, "Oh yeah, they went out. Carlie took that buggy of yours out with my wife." All I could think was, *Not the buggy!*

That night, the roads were wet from rain. I called her and called her—nothing. In the meantime, my panic was mounting. It had been an hour and I couldn't get her on the phone. With every passing minute, I was envisioning Carlie lying there dead in a wrecked buggy. I saw the slickness of the roads. I imagined the buggy rolling.

Weeks earlier, I'd rolled it myself, actually. A friend and I had taken it out on a wet field to perform power slides. All went fine. Then, he suggested getting out and filming me. But I didn't consider how an empty passenger seat would create an unsafe distribution of weight. I power slid without him and it rolled.

Thankfully, I'd been in a field and, other than giving myself a decent arm injury, I'd been fine. As the minutes ticked by without Carlie answering, I saw that buggy rolling again with Carlie inside. She wouldn't be so lucky. And I would end up a widower with three kids to raise on my own.

This wasn't a Volvo. It was a death trap!

Nothing Ashley feared actually happened. I was totally fine! His past experience of car accidents, however, started to warp his perspective and fear projected that crash onto me in the present. By the time I got home, he was in a state of panic. Even though nothing bad had happened, he was grieving as if it had.

The false pictures in Ashley's mind became more real to him than the facts of the situation. Fear shoved him from *What if something happens to Carlie?* straight to *Carlie's dead and I have three children to raise! I'll never make it all by myself!*

He was starting to operate on that false evidence, making plans based on a total lie.

EYES OF FAITH

When the spies returned from this mission to spy out the Promised Land, fear influenced their future:

> *They reported to him and said, "We came to the land where you sent us, and surely it flows with milk and honey, and this is the fruit of it. However, the people are strong that dwell in the land, and the cities are fortified and very great, and also we saw the children of Anak there"* (Numbers 13:27-28 MEV).

In other words, there were giants! This place had fortified cities and giants to guard them from invaders. To enter into that land and take possession of it as God had promised them would require ignoring what they saw with their physical eyes and seeing with eyes of faith. That was not something they were prepared to do.

Caleb listened to their faithless whimpering all he could stand. Then, in verse 30, *"Caleb silenced the people before Moses."* In other words, Caleb told them to "shut it!" God had promised them the land and what do they do? They doubt. They worry. They fear.

Here's something important worth noting: Caleb saw exactly what they saw. He was one of the spies, too. He toured the land of Canaan, saw the fortified cities, saw the giants. Anything they saw, he saw. But he viewed the situation through eyes of faith.

KICK OUT OLD TENANTS

Caleb silenced the people before Moses and said, *"Let us go up at once and possess it, for we are able to overcome it"* (Numbers 13:30 MEV).

The word "possess" here means to evict the previous tenants. Caleb was saying it was time to remove what no longer belonged and inhabit the land God had promised.

Do you have some old tenants who need to be kicked out? When we're moving into the future God has planned, we may need to first remove any squatters. Previous tenants in your life might be fear, doubt, unbelief, discouragement, pain, rejection, or abandonment—any negative emotions holding you back or creating torment. When it's time to possess our future, we may need to go in with force and evict what no longer belongs.

> ## WHEN IT'S TIME TO POSSESS OUR FUTURE, WE MAY NEED TO GO IN WITH FORCE AND EVICT WHAT NO LONGER BELONGS.

THE SPIRIT OF INSECURITY

When Caleb and Joshua returned with the other ten spies, they approached the situation with an entirely different spirit than the others. They spoke boldly, courageously, with hope and faith in their success and future.

The other ten spies spoke with fear:

> *But the men who had gone up with him said, "We are not able to go up against the people, for they are stronger than we." And they gave the children of Israel a bad report of the land which they had spied out, saying, "The land through which we have gone*

as spies is a land that devours its inhabitants, and all the people whom we saw in it are men of great stature. There we saw the giants (the descendants of Anak came from the giants); and we were like grasshoppers in our own sight, and so we were in their sight" (Numbers 13:31-33).

Nothing in their report confirms they'd actually witnessed any devouring going on. They did not see people being torn limb from limb. They imagined it. They looked at the size of the inhabitants and their insecurity filled in the rest.

If they had placed the rightful value on what God had already done for them in the past, they would have faced this new challenge with barely a shrug. Time after time, God had already led them to victory. He'd freed them from slavery. He'd defeated the Egyptians. He'd led them through the Red Sea.

If God wanted them to have this land, they would have it.

That's what they should have believed. Instead, they allowed insecurity to creep in and with it came defeating fear. The chosen people of God had forgotten who they were and replaced the reality of their victories with the fear of victimhood.

You can hear this clearly in the report as they begin describing the giants. *"In our eyes we were like grasshoppers, and so we were in their eyes"* (MEV). They were saying that the warriors were so much stronger and larger that it caused them to feel weak. Because they felt weak, they became weak.

THE REAL STORY

The warriors of Israel were not weak men. They were brave, strong soldiers. They were fighters, overcomers. They'd survived slavery, battles, challenges, and threats. They, also, were men of great stature.

Not only were they capable warriors, they'd been promised by God that the victory was theirs for the taking. The fight, in fact, was rigged. All they had to do was show up and they would win, but they weren't willing.

Caleb told them they would win. He assured them they were able, but they didn't believe him.

Years later, Rahab revealed that the Canaanites had been terrified of the Israelites ever since they heard of God parting the Red Sea! That's right. The giants were afraid of them! The truth of the situation, which Caleb had faith to see, was completely contrary to the fears of the other ten spies.

Have you ever been there? Has God made you a promise and you doubt it'll happen? Do you think God's promises are only for others? Do you doubt instead of believing and receiving?

LOOK OUTSIDE YOURSELF

Every promise of God is for every believer. His will is for you to be healthy, to have provision, to experience peace of mind. The lies of the enemy will say, "You are not able. It's not for you." But God has victory for you, if you'll only believe.

One of the most convincing ways fear traps us in an overwhelming challenge is by keeping us focused inwardly. We look at our own strength, our own capability, and we know we're not able. We look at the Anak giants and measure ourselves accordingly.

We, like them, miss the point. It was never going to be the children of Israel taking the Promised Land. It was always going to be God.

1 John 4:4 says, *"He who is in you is greater than he who is in the world."*

When we doubt that, we're doubting the power of God inside us. Whoever we are, whatever challenge we face, the power of God is stronger. The only thing holding us back from that Promised Land is our perception because the outcome was predetermined.

JUMPING THE HURDLES

In high school, I was always placed in the hurdle race. It made no sense. I'm all of five-foot nothing. I was the shortest kid in the whole school. Where the taller kids could sail over the hurdles with greater ease, I had a far bigger obstacle to get my legs over those boards.

To get me ready for the sprint, the coach started me off jumping small hurdles that were nearly flat on the floor. Like a twig. Each time I got over that small hurdle, the bar was raised for a higher hurdle. The more I trained, the more I jumped, the higher the bar raised until I got used to that obstacle in my way. Eventually, I was racing in a hundred-meter sprint and getting faster and smoother with each practice.

During the first race, I was running as fast as I could, and my knee smacked against one of the hurdles. It was excruciating. My knee swelled and bruised. It was a pain I'd not easily forget.

When it was time to return to training, I had to start all over again. And it didn't go well. I hit the first hurdle, the second, the third. It was demoralizing. I'd lost the ground I'd gained during all that practice. Even the things I could do before the race, I could no longer do. What was going on?

The coach saw my frustration and said, "Here's the problem. As you're running, you're remembering the pain of your knee striking that hurdle. You're carrying your past defeat into your future."

I was spending so much time focused on trying not to hit the hurdle, instead of jumping over it, that I was hitting it every time.

EYES ON THE PRIZE

Fear will always have you focusing on the wrong thing. We started this chapter with 1 Peter 5:7-9, and casting our cares upon the Lord. When we're confronting our fears, like that hurdle, we're taking our cares and anxiety on ourselves. We're trying to carry them, and the weight is keeping us burdened down. Before long, we grow weary and feel more like a victim than a victor.

That day, the coach gave me a great piece of advice. He said, "The only way to get past this is to focus on the finish line. You've got to look beyond the hurdle in front of you and keep your eyes on the finish line. When you do, you'll sail over that hurdle in front of you."

Does this ring true for you? Are you so focused on the disaster around you and the looming failure and the past pain that you've taken your eyes off your future victory?

Start looking forward with faith in where God is taking you. He has so much more for you than where you are right now. Stop dragging along past fears and rest in His love for you. He wants to lead you into your Promise Land. Keep your eyes on your victory that God's already won.

CHAPTER 7

FEAR IS A LOUSY PROVIDER

WILL GOD PROVIDE?

There are days, even after all this time in ministry, I still find myself asking, "Is this going to work out financially? Are we going to be okay?" It's a fear that can slip into a moment with barely any prompting. Our future always approaches with a pervasive question in mind: Will our needs be met?

The numbers on your bank statement can be solid, steady, and stable, yet you still feel unsettled. What you secretly, or even not-so-secretly, fear is lack. You worry you'll have needs that will go unmet. And it has nothing to do with your finances.

In fact, millionaires can be crippled with this lack mentality, while those with little means can be living freely with a prosperous outlook.

Circumstances have nothing to do with it. Fear does.

GOD'S PROMISE OF PROVISION

Our Heavenly Father understood this concern could burden and weigh us down. In Matthew 6, beginning in verse 25, He outlines His promise of provision, saying:

> *Therefore I say to you, do not worry about your life, what you will eat or what you will drink; nor about your body, what you will put on. Is not life more than food and the body more than clothing?*

Ashley always says that God is touching on the concerns of both men and women here. Men are always concerned with their stomachs. Women are usually concerned with their clothes. God is telling them both not to worry. He's aware of their needs.

> *Look at the birds of the air, for they neither sow nor reap nor gather into barns; yet your heavenly Father feeds them. Are you not of more value than they? Which of you by worrying can add one cubit to his stature? So why do you worry about clothing? Consider the lilies of the field, how they grow: they neither toil nor spin; and yet I say to you that even Solomon in all his glory was not arrayed like one of these. Now if God so clothes the grass of the field, which today is, and tomorrow is thrown into the oven, will He not much more clothe you, O you of little faith? Therefore*

do not worry, saying, 'What shall we eat?' or 'What shall we drink?' or 'What shall we wear?' For after all these things the Gentiles seek. For your heavenly Father knows that you need all these things. But seek first the kingdom of God and His righteousness, and all these things shall be added to you (Matthew 6:26-33).

That is no light promise. What Jesus is saying here is to not fear about your needs. Our Heavenly Father, our "Abba, Father," knows our needs intimately and He promises to provide.

There is only one thing on Earth that can block God's provision for us: us! If we'll let God provide for us, He will.

FAITH OF A CHILD

What God doesn't want is for us to fret and worry and wring our hands when times get rough. He wants us to be comforted in our assurance from Him that we'll never go hungry or be in desperate want.

Fear of lack can occupy our thoughts and steal our peace. Instead, God wants us resting and trusting that He will be our provider. He wants us exercising our childlike faith, which means taking the Word of God at face value and believing it.

It's that simple.

When you think about small children, do they worry about where their food is going to come from? Do they ever fret and ask, "Mommy, Daddy, will you feed me today? Will you clothe me today? Will you pay the mortgage or rent today so that I have a place to sleep?"

No, they simply believe what they need will be provided. They trust a good parent to continue being a good parent.

God is our good, good Father. He is trustworthy and His love for us is trustworthy. We can count on Him to provide for our needs far better than we can provide for our needs. He has promised to always look after us. All we have to do is take Him at His Word.

AFRAID TO SCATTER

Fear in your finances actually hinders how you operate. It affects how you give and how you trust God. When you see a need you feel prompted to help support financially, that voice in your head will remind you of all your bills, all your coming expenses, and have you doing math instead of trusting God.

"You can't afford to give," fear will say. "If you give, how are you going to meet your needs?"

Those are the lies fear whispers in your ear. If you haven't got your financial security in God settled in your heart, if you doubt God's love for you, if you question whether or not He'll provide, that fear will stop you from acting on God's prompting.

You'll find yourself listening to that voice of fear instead of the voice of faith.

Proverbs 11:24 says, *"There is one who scatters, yet increases more; and there is one who withholds more than is right but it leads to poverty."* This means that our tight grasp on our money actually leads to less. It leads to a fear mentality.

Faith, however, says, "God will provide for me when I give." When we give freely, faithfully, and without fear, it comes back to us.

GO AND POSSESS IT

Matthew 6 shares the promise that God will provide. However, it isn't an excuse for laziness. When it becomes a reason to sit around and do nothing, while waiting for money to magically appear, we've taken the scripture beyond the meaning.

A few years ago, Ashley was ministering to a young man who had come to us for guidance due to his money troubles. He was broke and approaching a dire situation. To help him get on his feet, Ashley offered to help him find a job. His response to the offer of work was, "No, no. God is going to provide for me."

This man pushed God's promise of provision out of balance. Yes, God is going to provide. That doesn't mean nothing is required out of us to receive that provision. This man refused to possess what God was providing.

Deuteronomy 8:18 says that God gives us the power to gain wealth. This is not a promise to be lazy. It's a promise that our work, our labor, will never be in vain. We can be at ease as we labor, knowing we are free from the curse of useless, meaningless toil. When we put our hands to something, God will prosper it as we work.

Yes, God is going to provide. Many times, His provision comes in the form of labor for our hands.

Let's go back to the story of the Promised Land we talked about in the previous chapter. God gave the children of Israel the land. Then, He commanded them to "go and possess it."

God provided for them. They didn't have to find the land. They wouldn't be fighting the battles on their own strength. They never needed to be anxious over the challenges that awaited in seizing God's promise. They did, however, need to go in and possess it.

For us, the same guidance applies. We don't need to fret and be anxious over our finances. We need to trust that God has a plan to provide, then ask Him to point us in the right direction. If we're struggling financially, we can ask God for work, for extra hours, for new business ideas, for new career directions. He is there to guide us toward His provision, while blessing the labor He provides for our hands.

It's never *if* God is going to provide for us. It's *how*.

IT'S NEVER *IF* GOD IS GOING TO PROVIDE FOR US. IT'S *HOW*.

MONEY IN THE FLOORBOARDS

When Ashley and I moved across the country to attend Bible college, we knew it was led by the Lord. It wasn't easy to move away from family and start this new chapter, but we followed God's prompting and trusted He would make a way.

We rented a house, enrolled in college, and put all three kids in school, too. All of that, of course, required money. With us both in school, money wasn't something abundantly flowing. And, at that stage in our faith walk, we'd gotten it in our heads that we were going to be so spiritual we wouldn't need to work. God would make it all happen effortlessly.

We hadn't really thought it through, obviously.

As we were trying to figure out how to make this new chapter work, we hit a financial wall. Our resources had run dry and rent was due in days.

We were in a bit of a pickle. Yet, in spite of us, God was still so gracious.

At that time, I remember leaning on Philippians 4:19 so heavily, which says, *"And my God shall supply all your need according to His riches in glory by Christ Jesus."* That was the scripture I'd stood on when deciding to make this major change, and it was the scripture I took to God one day while vacuuming.

"God, remember You gave me a promise to stand on? Well, I know you're not usually early, but it'd be really nice if You weren't late. The rent's due." I vacuumed and prayed in tongues and waited for the Lord to answer and He did. He told me, "I've already provided for you."

He had? Great! So…where was it?

As I'm vacuuming and praying, the vacuum hit the baseboard near the front door where the mail comes in, and out slipped a check. It had fallen and been hidden in the wall cavity for two months. The amount covered our rent that month and the next!

God is always faithful. Again, it was never *if* He would provide, it was *how*.

We actually went through Bible college debt free. God provided. He worked in so many ways, including opening up opportunities for Ashley to buy and sell products for our income.

Being lazy, sitting and doing nothing, would have blocked God's provision. He called us to cooperate with His plans. To go and possess the blessings and provisions He has waiting. He called us to not worry. To not be anxious. To ask. To trust. To cooperate.

Our needs will be met, which is why there's never any reason to fear.

REAL SECURITY

Whether we have abundant resources or not, the fear of lack can still influence our outlook. The presence or absence of fear is not based on our bank accounts. It's based on our focus.

In Mark 10, we learn of a rich young ruler. He was a man with everything. He had power. He had money. And he even still had his youth. This rich young ruler, a man with the world in the palm of his hand, approached Jesus with admiration. In verse 21, it says, *"Then Jesus, looking at him, loved him."*

This is important to note because of the direction Jesus was about to give this young man. Even though it seemed like a hard ask, it was done in love. It was for his own good.

"One thing you lack," Jesus continued. He gave this young man a heads up that there was something in him that needed to be addressed. *"Go your way, sell whatever you have, and give to the poor, and you will have treasure in heaven; and come, take up the cross, and follow Me"* (Mark 10:21).

How did the young man respond?

"But he was sad at this word, and went away sorrowful, for he had great possessions" (Mark 10:22). He couldn't let go of his wealth. He had it in abundance, but losing it created a fear of lack.

This man trusted in his wealth, not in God. He believed his needs wouldn't be met if he followed Jesus. He trusted the wrong source for his peace and provision.

In Mark 4:1-20, Jesus told the parable of the sower. He said that there are three things that choke the Word and make it unfruitful in our lives: the cares of this world, the deceitfulness of riches, and the desires for other things.

For that rich young ruler, his belief that wealth was what gave him security choked out the fruitfulness of the Word in his life. He wanted to follow Jesus, but he believed the lie that tangible finances were more secure than being in God's will.

Due to his fear of lack, he went away sorrowful, and it kept him from following Jesus. That's what fear will do to all of us. It will pull us away from our relationship with God.

GIVE AWAY YOUR FEAR

When fear creeps into the realm of our finances, it can hinder us from taking opportunities or blessings God has planned for us.

For Ashley and me, one of the things we've found as a path to victory over fear is being obedient when the Lord prompts us to give. We've come to recognize that when God asks us to give—to missionaries, other ministries, organizations, or simply just benevolent giving—if our first response is hesitation, it is because of fear. The only way to silence that fear is to give anyway!

The rich young ruler could have overcome his fear, too. He could have taken all those precious possessions and given them away. But, instead, the wealthy man gave in to his fear of lack.

NO FEAR IN GIVING

Reading further in Mark, we find a completely different story concerning finances. Jesus is at the synagogue where people are coming up and giving.

Now Jesus sat opposite the treasury and saw how the people put money into the treasury. And many who were rich put in much (Mark 12:41).

Imagine this for a moment: Your pastor is standing there watching how much people are giving. We've attended a church like this, actually, with offering plates at the front. Once during the offering, a man walked up and left money in one of the plates. As he walked off, the pastor said, "Hey, come back. You can do better than that."

Can you imagine if that happened? Can you imagine how uncomfortable that would be? Well, that's what was happening. Jesus was sitting there seeing how much people were giving.

But, for Jesus, it isn't about the amounts. It's about the faith. It's about what we give in comparison to what we have. That's what He was bringing to everyone's attention.

While there, a woman with very little made a donation.

Then one poor widow came and threw in two mites, which make a quadrans. So He called His disciples to Himself and said to them, "Assuredly, I say to you that this poor widow has put in more than all those who have given to the treasury; for they all put in out of their abundance, but she out of her poverty put in all that she had, her whole livelihood (Mark 12:42-44).

She gave two mites, which makes a quadrans. How much is this? At most, it was roughly two to three dollars. It was nearly nothing, yet it was all she had. When Jesus saw this, He called the disciples to Himself for a teaching moment. If anyone had a reason to fear, it was the widow woman. She had nothing, but she still gave. She chose faith over fear.

THE BIGGEST GIVER

This poor woman's faith got the Savior's attention. He pointed to her as an example to emulate. He commended her for her giving and her faith. In 2 Corinthians 9:7, it says that God loves a cheerful giver. It's almost as if Jesus couldn't help Himself. He had to say something about her.

I can't wait to meet this woman in Heaven. I have no doubt she has a mind-blowing testimony of God's provision from that day on.

GOD WILL ALWAYS BE THE BIGGEST GIVER.

When we give generously, it so delights God that He lavishes blessings back onto us. God will always be the biggest giver.

However, if fear hinders us from giving, we could be leading our lives into a lack situation. Like Proverbs 11:24 says, the one who withholds more than is right thinks they're protecting themselves from being in need, but they ultimately lead themselves into poverty.

FEAR CREATES IMBALANCE

Fear of lack not only influences our financial status, it tips over into other areas as well. When we allow greed into our lives, we're also opening the door to other sins, such as gluttony.

Greed and gluttony often go hand-in-hand. When you fear your needs will not be met, you can begin looking at food with fear, too. Instead of being grateful for what's been provided, you fear it may not come again. So, you overindulge. You eat everything you can. You struggle to share and to balance your actual needs.

The same lie powers greed, gluttony, hoarding, and sometimes stealing: You're going to run out. Get as much as you can now because there's no guarantee more will be available later.

This can manifest anywhere you have abundance. You do not need to be in actual want for this fear to take hold and become irrational.

REGAIN YOUR CONTROL

If you're operating in fear and see imbalance happening in your life, you can stop this. You start by repenting, by changing your mind. Tell God about your fear and how you don't want it driving your life anymore.

This will always be God's will for your life. He does not want you operating in fear. He has better for you. He has faith for you. He wants you operating in the promises He's given you. He will provide (praise God!) if you let Him. To do that, we simply believe His promises.

When we believe God's promises, we act on God's promises. One of the greatest aspects of practicing our faith with our finances is that it's a tangible action. We can give and act in faith. As James says, "*So also faith, if it does not have works (deeds and actions of obedience to back it up), by itself is destitute of power (inoperative, dead)*" (James 2:17 AMPC).

That is how you silence the fear of lack. You give.

When we do, we're showing God that we're putting Him first. We're trusting Him. We're living out of faith instead of living out of fear. We're telling our natural circumstances that they don't get the final say. You'll be amazed how you can prosper with this action.

It is more blessed to give than to receive (Acts 20:35). Start giving and see the blessings and provisions God has set aside for you.

134

CHAPTER 8

BREAKING THE FEAR HABIT

WILL YOU OVERCOME?

Fear can be beaten. I say this because I've done it. As I've shared in multiple examples, Ashley and I have made plenty of our own mistakes with fear! So, fear is something I can speak about, not from the outside, but from the eye of the storm.

I get it. My husband and I both understand this battle, but we've also seen God use this battle to teach us how to overcome. And that's what I want for you, too. I want to see you overcome.

Never forget: God has given us a spirit of power, of love, and of a sound mind. Those are His promises to His children. We can trust those promises are there for the taking. God made a promise, and He never breaks a promise. Not ever. Not with anyone. Even if your circumstances try to convince you otherwise. God promises victory over fear.

FEAR'S UNGODLY INFLUENCE

One of the most destructive effects of living in fear is that is creates a pattern of unbelief. When fear comes, it drags doubt and torment along with it. We find ourselves stuck, frozen, unable to move forward.

Faith is what frees our feet. With faith, we find strength, energy, and the courage to advance. Faith brings increase, and that's where we want to be living with God every single day.

So, what does living fearlessly look like?

As we've talked about in previous chapters, fearlessness means being bold, intrepid, and courageous. Doesn't that sound amazing? That's the kind of life God has called us to live. He wants us to stand on the edge of that deep, cavernous fear and not even blink. He wants us to feel empowered through Him and to face whatever life brings with security and confidence in our position in Christ.

Fear will always prey on our insecurity. That is its home turf. Its ground zero. It thrives in any insecurity we allow to creep in. God, however, wants us secure in His love for us, secure in His care for us, and secure in His authority in our lives. This is how we crush and overpower the lies that lead to insecurity.

PRACTICAL STEPS OUT OF FEAR

If you've recognized fear operating in your life, I have good news for you. There's an antidote. You can overcome. Here's how:

I. RECOGNIZE THE PATTERN

Fear creates a pattern of unbelief. Think of fear and unbelief as bosom pals. One doesn't like to be without the other. They are intertwined and deeply connected. When fear goes unchecked, it invites its buddy.

Hebrews 4:11 says, *"Let us labor therefore to enter that rest, lest anyone fall by the same pattern of unbelief.* (MEV).

Unbelief then hinders God's work in our lives. Unbelief, in fact, hindered Jesus from performing miracles.

2. COOPERATE WITH GOD

As we discussed in an earlier chapter, Jesus dealt with unbelief by removing Himself and the blind man out of the city. There was so much unbelief there, Jesus' mighty works had little to no effect on the people. In order to heal the blind man, He took him away from the unbelief.

Jesus was able to heal the man. Jesus is *always* able, but God has given us free will. He needs our cooperation in order for the power of God to flow. Otherwise, we hinder ourselves from accessing all God has for us.

God has already provided everything we need, but if we don't believe that, we won't receive His provision.

3. BELIEVE RIGHT

You have a choice to make. You can believe God for good, or you can doubt. You can allow past experiences, trauma, difficult circumstances, and any number of negative influences to convince you the fear is real. But, remember the FEAR acronym: False Evidence Appearing Real.

Don't believe the lie. Don't allow fear to grow and cultivate that lie until it becomes a mountain. Don't let that false evidence change your perception of things. Don't let fear be the authority that makes your decisions.

Instead, believe Him for good.

4. CHOOSE LIFE

Jesus specifically told us, "Do not fear." All throughout the Gospels, He repeated those words to His disciples, to the sick, to anyone who approached Him. "Do not fear," He urged. "Do not fear," He encouraged. "Do not fear," He commanded.

He isn't asking something of us we can't do. He gives us the ability to do exactly as He instructed. He gives us the power not to fear.

In Deuteronomy 30:19, God said, *"I have set before you life and death…therefore choose life"*

God has given you the power to turn from fear and choose life. All you have to do is believe Him.

BREAK THE FEAR HABIT

One of the biggest hurdles stopping us from living a fearless life is the fact fear has become a habit. We've lived with fear for so long it feels normal, natural. We can even find the familiarity of it comfortable. Responding to circumstances with fear becomes our go-to reaction. It's what we've always done, so we just keep doing it.

> **WE'VE LIVED WITH FEAR FOR SO LONG IT FEELS NORMAL, NATURAL. WE CAN EVEN FIND THE FAMILIARITY OF IT COMFORTABLE.**

We have to break that habit.

Breaking bad habits and unrealized patterns is hard work. It will take purposeful, intentional warfare. It may even take a stinging reminder. At least it did for me.

A few years ago, I recognized a negative habit in my life: I was sarcastic. The retorts and responses…let's just say they came naturally. My language could, at times, be biting. And I didn't like it.

So, to break the habit, I wore a rubber band around my wrist. Every time I caught myself slipping into sarcasm, I'd snap that rubber band against the soft, delicate part of my wrist. And, yes, it hurt!

Sounds barbaric, right?

What I knew was that breaking this damaging habit of mine took a change of action. I needed a wake-up call. I needed to snap out of it. So, I literally snapped myself out of it.

To get rid of the negative pattern of fearful thinking, we must first recognize fear has become our habit. One of the indicators is that we'll see that pattern appear in our speech.

Scripture tells us that out of the abundance of the heart, the mouth speaks (Luke 6:45). We have to pay attention to what is appearing and reappearing in our speech. What are our predominant thoughts? Are they doubting? Are they hopeless? Do they expect the worst instead of the best?

If this is what our mouths are confessing, this is what our hearts are possessing.

POSITIVE BELIEF

Once we've identified our habit, the most important step in breaking it is addressing our unbelief. We will never overcome our fear until we choose to believe what the Word of God says about our situation.

Our belief can't be based on what our bodies are telling us, what the doctors are telling us, what the circumstances are telling us, or what it looks like in the natural realm. Our belief must be through our confidence in what the Word of God says.

Psalm 17:13 says, *"I believe I will see the goodness of the Lord in the land of the living"* (MEV). The psalmist is placing his trust in the goodness of God. In other words, he is saying, "I trust the Word of God above my circumstances."

When we do that, when we place our trust in God's goodness, we will begin to see that goodness all around us. We'll see good in places where we previously only saw negative.

One of the characteristics of fear is negativity. As we've all experienced, it's difficult to be around negative people. They drain us of energy. Even after they're gone, the negativity lingers.

Positive people, on the other hand, are always a delight. We could be around them all day.

This difference is crucial to recognize so that we continually push against any victim mentality trying to form and, instead, embrace a victor mentality. When we choose to believe God is good, that He loves us, and that His promises are for us, we can rest in His provisional care for us, whether that's financially, emotionally, spiritually, or physically.

THE WAITING GAME

When we look back at Psalms 27:13-14 in the New King James Version, it says, *"I would have lost heart, unless I had believed that I would see the goodness of the Lord in the land of the living. Wait on the Lord; be of good courage, and he shall strengthen your heart."*

God is showing us the path to strengthening our heart and living courageously: Choose to believe and then wait.

And that's where the glitch happens, doesn't it? We're waiting on God to do something, aren't we? That waiting often feels like being stuck at a bus stop waiting for our ride. Will the bus come or won't it? Will God move or won't He?

The waiting part feels undecided. Even risky. We wait, and the doubt and unbelief and fear creep back in.

That's why it's important to understand the meaning here. The word "wait" in this instance means more than simply hanging around waiting for something to happen. It means looking expectantly for the moment when something will happen. It's a hopeful, eager wait. It's not standing at the bus stop wondering when the bus arrives, it's looking down the road for the first glimpse that it's on its way to you.

Don't miss this point. It's powerful and necessary. If we're going to break a pattern of unbelief, we must choose to believe the Word of God and to wait on God with positive expectancy. To be of good courage. To be constant, firm footed, steadfast, and immovable in our belief in the goodness of God.

MEDITATE DAY AND NIGHT

Ashley and I have experienced moments in our lives where we've had to choose to believe God over our circumstances, then steadfastly stand there. And wait. During those times, we needed the Word of God constantly in front of our eyes.

Like Joshua 1:8 says, *"This Book of the Law shall not depart from your mouth, but you shall meditate in it day and night."* We meditated on God's goodness without ceasing, and it left no room for fear and anxiety.

If this sounds difficult, know that God has given all of us the ability to meditate on His Words, promises, and goodness. This is a choice. We're going to have thoughts circling through our minds throughout the day. If there's something causing us concern, we somehow manage to go about our daily routine and still *worry* without ceasing, right? But what if we replaced that worry with belief? What if, instead of meditating on our anxiety or difficult circumstances, we meditate on the goodness of God?

FIND YOUR PROMISE

Years ago, while living in London, Ashley and I were facing a fearful situation that needed our complete attention focused on God's promises. We needed to meditate on God's Word day and night.

So, we went to the store, bought a bunch of sticky notes, wrote scriptures on them, and plastered them all over our flat.

They were everywhere. Feeling hungry? There were God's promises on the refrigerator. Time to brush your teeth? God's promises were there at the bathroom sink, staring us in the face. We were brainwashing ourselves, truly washing our brains, with the truth. It was everywhere we turned.

Meditating on Scripture day and night does not mean sitting in the center of the room with your legs crossed, eyes closed, and chanting. It means continually keeping God's Word at the forefront of our minds. It could be a verse, many verses, or even a single word. Focus on the truth of God's Word and see what the Holy Spirit shows you.

Think on it, speak it, utter it out loud. Meditating means to speak, study, utter, or roar like a lion. When's the last time you roared Scripture like a lion?

When you're facing a challenge, when fear is growing by leaps and bounds inside you, seek out scriptures you are choosing to stand on during this trial and write them down. Go sticky note crazy like we did, if it helps. However you choose to do it, keep the Word of God before your eyes and declare it over your life.

ASKED AND ANSWERED

When we look back at Joshua 1:8 again, it goes on to say, *"Meditate in it day and night, that you may observe to do according to all that is written in it."*

God is giving us healthy instruction here. We're not the ones making things happen. God has already provided for us, but we're instructed to observe all God tells us to do so we can receive the things God has already provided.

Does that mean if we focus and study and roar that God will bless us?

No. It means God has already blessed us. He's already provided. God is a good father who has provided all that we need. Every precious promise is yes and amen (2 Corinthians 1:20). Meditating on the truth that His promises are for us—that they're already provided and guaranteed by Christ's death, burial, and resurrection—is how we see those promises come about in our lives.

The promise of provision? This is how we see it. The promise of healing? This is how we see it.

When we were born again, we were joined with Jesus in spirit. 1 John 4:17 says, *"As He is, so are we in this world."* Colossians 2:10 says, *"You are complete in Him."* So, we already have everything we need. The question is, are we seeing it in our everyday lives?

> WHEN WE MEDITATE ON THE TRUTH THAT GOD'S PROMISES ARE GUARANTEED, WE SEE THEM COME ABOUT IN OUR LIVES.

THE MOUTH MAGNIFIES

At times, we can be speaking words of unbelief, thoughts not based on Scripture, and not even realize it until someone points it out. Has that ever happened to you? Has a friend ever remarked on your negativity? Has anyone ever bluntly called you out on your toxicity?

Not everyone has friends who will. When they do, however, it pays to listen.

Years ago, we had two people who were temporarily living with us: a 17-year-old young man attending Bible school and a 70-year-old woman serving as our children's nanny. Both in different phases of life. Both struggling. Both speaking unbelief over their lives and not seeing it.

One day, we were all in the car, and she was talking about all these health issues she "knew" were going to happen to her because, "They always happen to me." Meanwhile, he was talking about money concerns and how it was "impossible" to get a good job and get ahead.

Ashley took all he could take until he finally had enough. He stopped the car and said, "I'm done with this. You're living in my house. And in my house, we don't speak sickness and we don't speak poverty. If you're sick, we're going to pray for you and believe the best for you. If you're lacking financially, we're going to pray for you and believe the best for you. We're going to stop giving voice to the problems and start giving voice to the solution."

Whatever we voice, whatever we focus on, whatever we magnify, gets bigger. So, we have a decision to make. Are we going to grow our problems? Or grow our hopeful expectancy?

Psalm 34:3 says, *"Oh, magnify the Lord with me, and let us exalt His name together."*

After Ashely had his "come to Jesus" talk with our guests, things started to change. Their language changed, their mindsets changed, their focus changed from unbelief to belief. And, yes, their circumstances changed within a few short months!

This is why it's important to check what we are believing. If we allow fear in, then that becomes our focus and it begins to magnify. The power of that fear over us strengthens, and we're hindered from receiving God's promises.

DON'T EMPOWER THE LIE

When I was thirty-weeks pregnant with our daughter, Hannah, we received a horrible report from the doctor. After a sonogram, the doctor called Ashley and I into the office and broke the bad news. He told us that half of Hannah's brain was missing and her hands had not formed correctly.

Then he asked us, "So what would you like to do about your pregnancy?"

"My pregnancy?" I shot back not too politely. "This isn't a pregnancy. This is a baby! I'm thirty weeks along, don't you call this a 'pregnancy.'" And I sort of huffed out of the office.

On the car ride home, Ashley and I were silent. We didn't talk about the horrible news we'd just received. We didn't consider our options. We didn't make plans for caring for an infant with a partially formed brain and body.

It's was like we both knew we couldn't give voice to that fear. We couldn't empower the fear by letting it out of our mouths. We weren't being particularly spiritual about it at that point, but we seemed to realize that speaking this forth would only have disastrous results.

Weeks later, I gave birth to a beautiful little girl with two fully formed hands and a fully formed brain. Praise Jesus!

FEAR AT THE DOOR

Fear is sneaky. It always has been. It always will be. It doesn't always need to enter into your life and your thinking through the front door. There's always a backdoor, a window, or a crack in the foundation to slither up through.

That's why guarding its entrance takes diligence and aware-ness. Are we paying attention to what we're feeding our hearts and minds? What we're watching? What we're listening to? Who we're around? Fear won't always announce itself when it arrives. It can even come through in areas or sources that are good or, at the very least, neutral.

For example, are you a person who watches the nightly news? How does that affect you? Do you still feel peaceful and calm after? Or are you yelling your frustrations at your television screen?

Staying informed is good. We don't want to cut ourselves off from the world. But, if your news watching is creating stress and anxiety, then it's not producing good fruit. It may be time to turn it off.

Another seemingly innocuous example might be Christian music.

I know what you're thinking: *But Christian music is good*! It can be. And it cannot be. Just because a song is categorized as "Christian," or played on a Christian station, does not mean it is sharing biblical truth. There are many lyrics in Christian music that are simply not based in the Word of God. Be dil-igent. Pay attention to what you're hearing, especially when your defenses are down. That's when fear likes to strike.

Another example, of course, is the friends and family in your life. If you're the only believer in your family, you're deal-ing with this openly and frequently. Fear will be easier to spot then because you're more guarded.

However, many times we can be exposed to fearful thinking through people at church. They may be struggling with unbelief in their lives, or speaking unbelief openly, and it can start to influence you because you're more open to listening to fellow Christians.

In times like these, we must encourage ourselves. David did this frequently, like in Psalm 103:1 where he wrote, *"Bless the Lord, O my soul; and all that is within me, bless His holy name!"*

Feed yourself. Go where you can find Godly encouragement and truth. Find people and places where you can *"exalt His name together."* Be picky about what you hear so that fear never even finds wiggle room.

CONCLUSION

Living fearlessly can feel like a battle for the ages. You may have reached a point where it feels as if a certain amount of fear will always be with you. But, I'm here to tell you it doesn't have to be that way.

I think you know that.

You picked up this book because a fearless life is the life you want. And God desires, more than you can possibly know, to give you that life. He can, if you'll only trust Him. If you'll only take Him at His Word. Jesus died to give you that freedom. Will you accept it?

As you face the current and future challenges in your life, I want to leave you with this final scripture and thought. We're going back to David because he was a man who suffered great hardships, faced many threats, struggled many times, but always returned to the source of all comfort—his Heavenly Father.

In Psalm 34:1, David gives us guidance on what to do when we don't know what to do: *"I will bless the Lord at all times; His praise shall be continually be in my mouth."*

When you feel defeated, praise God.

When you feel hopeless, praise God.

When you feel lost for direction, praise God.

When you feel full of fear, praise God.

Worship invites the power of God into our situations. It's that powerful. Praise is verbalizing truth because God is always worthy of praise. He is always good. Regardless of our situations, we can always find something to praise God about.

With praise, we are choosing belief. We're choosing to take control of our thinking. King David continued in Psalm 34:2-4, *"My soul shall make its boast in the Lord; The humble shall hear of it and be glad. Oh, magnify the Lord with me, And let us exalt His name together. I sought the Lord, and He heard me, And delivered me from all my fears."*

If you're looking for deliverance from your fears today, you can find that deliverance in the arms of God. That is where you'll find fearless living. That is where you'll find the boldness and courage to live freely, as God always intended for your life.

It is available for you right now in this moment.

Now that we've come to the end of our fearless journey together, I want to leave you with a prayer. Quiet your mind. Rest in God's love. And pray this with me for a life of fearlessness:

Father God, I thank You for calling us to live a life that's free from fear. You give us authority over our fear so we don't have to live with it a moment longer. And I praise You for that.

Right now, I invite You to come into my heart. I receive your deliverance, Jesus. Let this confession bring glory to You, Lord.

I repent of all the words I have spoken out in fear. I ask that those fearful, unbelieving words be uprooted right now, in Jesus' name.

I agree with Your Word, Lord. I magnify Your truth above all my fear, all my negativity, all my past experiences, and all the reports coming against me. I take my thoughts captive, in Jesus' name. I lay them at Your feet. I declare that Your perfect love casts out all my fear, in Jesus' name.

Amen.

MY FEARLESS DECLARATION

I am who He says I am.

I have what He says I have.

I can do what He says I can do.

I have all the money I need,

all the resources I need,

all the favor I need,

all the opportunity I need,

all the time I need

to do everything God has called me to do.

I do not lack for inspiration.

I do not lack for vision.

I do not lack for wisdom.

I do not lack for understanding.

I have the mind of Christ.
I have the Holy Spirit
who brings all things back to my remembrance
and leads me into all truth.
I have the peace of God,
the presence of God,
the power of God,
the purpose of God,
and the protection of God working in my life.
My path is clear.
My direction is set.
My destination is certain.
My heart is steadfast.
My eyes are fixed and my word is sent.
I am fully persuaded that
He who began a good work in me will complete it,
He is perfecting those things which concern me,
He is working all things together for my good,
calling those things which be not as though they are.
I believe, therefore I receive
every good thing which He has set aside for me today!

ABOUT THE AUTHOR

CARLIE TERRADEZ is an international speaker, author, wife and mother of three amazing children. Born and raised in the United Kingdom, her family immigrated to the United States after she and her husband, Ashley, graduated from Bible college in 2008.

Shortly after her ordination, she became the co-founder of Terradez Ministries, a practical teaching ministry dedicated to empowering believers to walk in God's power and promises.

Carlie's life is a testimony to the miraculous power of God. She has been supernaturally healed from numerous life-threatening conditions, including epilepsy, and has also seen her terminally ill three-year-old daughter instantly recover. Carlie is passionate about helping others receive healing and walk in the abundant life that Jesus has provided for them.

The Harrison House Vision

Proclaiming the truth and the power
of the Gospel of Jesus Christ with excellence.
Challenging Christians
to live victoriously,
grow spiritually,
know God intimately.

Connect with us on

![f] Facebook @ HarrisonHousePublishers
and ![Instagram] Instagram @ HarrisonHousePublishing
so you can stay up to date with news
about our books and our authors.

Visit us at **www.harrisonhouse.com**
for a complete product listing as well as
monthly specials for wholesale distribution.